Help from
The Little Red Hen

Reversing Poverty with Responsibility

by Stephen Gibson

ISBN: 978-1-934447-83-3

Published by:
Whispering Pines Publishing
11013 Country Pines Road
Shoals, Indiana 47581
www.countrypinesprinting.com

Help from

The Little Red Hen

Reversing Poverty with Responsibility

About the Author

Stephen Gibson has served as international director of Holiness Pilgrim Missions since January, 2011.

Gibson is married, with six children and seven grandchildren.

His previous ministry included pastoring, foreign mission work, Bible college teaching and administration, Christian school teaching and administration, and writing.

He lived in Ukraine with his family for five years and served Kiev Wesley Bible College in the roles of professor, academic dean, and president. During that time he also taught classes at other colleges and preached in churches in Ukraine and Russia.

He has taught at Union Bible College and Allegheny Wesleyan College, and is currently a part-time professor at God's Bible School & College in Cincinnati. His courses include intercultural studies and urban ministry.

He graduated from Union Bible College with a Th.B., from Wesley Biblical Seminary with an M.A. in Theology, from Louisiana Baptist University with an M.A. in Biblical Studies, and from Grace Theological Seminary with a D.Min.

He is ordained by the Pilgrim Holiness Church. Gibson pastored Victory Chapel, a diverse inner-city church in Indianapolis, for five years.

Books written by Gibson include *The Prosperity Prophets* (English & Russian); *Steps of Grace* (Russian, English, & French); *The Sincerity of God: A Demonstration of the Wesleyan Promise Hermeneutic;* and *Practical Christianity*, a course for discipleship (English, Russian, & Chinese).

Books edited by Gibson include *I Believe: Fundamentals of the Christian Faith* and *A Timeless Faith: John Wesley for the 21st Century.*

His most recent book is *Help from The Little Red Hen: Reversing Poverty with Responsibility.*

He is a writer for Shepherd's Global Classroom, preparing courses for ministry training worldwide. His courses include *Christian Beliefs, Cults and World Religions, Church Issues, Romans,* and *Ministry Leadership.*

Contents

Part 1:

The Poverty Scene

Chapter 1
What Is Poverty?

Devon knew that his parents could not choose to live in another neighborhood. In the United States, when millions of blacks moved north, cities built apartment complexes for families who could not afford to rent houses in ordinary neighborhoods. The "projects" quickly became known for vandalism, violence, and crime. Everyone in "the projects" was automatically considered poor, because nobody was there who could afford to be elsewhere.

Who is poor? Many people think themselves poor in comparison to others. Some who profess poverty would be considered rich by people in worse circumstances.

A dictionary definition could be as follows: "The state or condition of having little or no money, goods, or means of support." Further defined, it is "a state of privation and lack of necessities." It is a "serious lack of the means for proper existence."

> **Poverty is a denial of choices and opportunities.**

The United Nations has defined poverty more extensively:

Fundamentally, poverty is a denial of choices and opportunities, a violation of human dignity. It means lack of basic capacity to participate effectively in society. It means not having enough to feed and clothe a family, not having a school or clinic to go to, not having the land on which to grow one's food or a job to earn one's living, not having access to credit. It means insecurity, powerlessness and exclusion of individuals, households and communities. It means susceptibility to violence, and it often implies living in marginal or fragile environments, without access to clean water or sanitation.[1]

The above definition, or description, gives details that tend to go together in circumstances of poverty. A person could be considered impoverished even if his situation doesn't include all those details. For example, a person who has shelter and food but needs medical care and cannot afford it is in poverty.

Poverty should be defined in terms of essential needs rather than by various levels of optional spending. For example, a person who can travel adequately by bus is not impoverished because of being unable to buy a car. A person who is getting sufficient nourishment is not impoverished because of not being able to buy the food he prefers. To say that a person is in poverty compared to someone else is to misunderstand what poverty essentially is.

To be in poverty is to be without something essential. Poverty means that the lack of a missing essential is painfully felt.

Essentials are things usually taken for granted by people who have always had them. Those people may think they struggle financially, but they are struggling for more security, a higher level of prosperity, or improved convenience, or even preferred entertainment. They are not struggling with the lack of something essential.

Bertram dreaded the walk home from school every day, because it was like running a gauntlet. If caught by the roaming gangs of older boys, he would be shoved and cuffed, possibly getting his clothes torn. His teachers had no idea of the anxiety that seethed in his mind as he sat in class every afternoon, trying to think of a new way to sneak home. There was no man among his neighbors that he could hope would notice and intervene. His mother would be at Taco Bell, where she would work

1   United Nations statement, June, 1998.

9

late. Bertram could not even imagine living in a place where he would not be afraid of his neighbors.

Chapter 2
The Origin of the "Inner City"

If you drive into a large city from the suburbs, not getting on bypasses or interstate highways that cut through the city, but staying on city streets, you see how neighborhoods change as you go further in.

The suburbs around the edge may be communities formed by developers, where the streets, sidewalks, and parks are all new. Or they may be small towns that were enveloped by the city, but have managed to keep a distinct identity.

As you go further in, the houses and neighborhoods are older. Some of them are still considered good neighborhoods; after all, they were once suburbs also. You may see streets of grand old houses that are well maintained.

The last type of area you enter before getting to the downtown business area is called the "inner city." This is what is called "the bad part of town." Diagramed, the inner city would be like a doughnut around the expensive downtown business area. A property you could not buy for $10,000,000 may be only twenty blocks from a property you could not sell for $10,000.

So how did the inner city become as it is?

Natural City Development

There were some natural stages of city development that created the inner city, especially in large cities in the United States.

When the only transportation was by shipping or horse-drawn vehicles, most business and manufacturing needed to be downtown. Production was limited by the difficulty of bringing together supplies, sending out products, and getting workers onto the site daily. Therefore, suppliers, manufacturers, and sellers could all benefit by being close to one another. The businesses most centrally located had the greatest profit potential, so central land was very valuable. As the business area grew, residences in the area were leveled or remodeled for commercial use.

Most employment was downtown. Since workers needed to travel from home to work every day, either by horse-drawn street cars or on foot, they needed to live near the downtown business district. Soon a large residential area of working-class people ringed the business district.

Business owners and the wealthy soon preferred not to live in the area becoming crowded with working class people. They moved outside the area for more comfortable living. Nobody in the area could afford to rent or buy the fine homes they left behind, so those houses were divided into rental units.

As the social class of the area continued to drop, those who could afford to move out of the crowded, now lower-class area did so, leaving behind an even poorer average population. The empty spaces were usually filled with immigrants who were looking for employment and could afford nothing better.

Because of the high cost of land and the low income of the population, a property could be used for residence only if used intensively, crowded with occupants who were paying low rent.

Their large rooms were partitioned into several smaller ones (without regard to proper light or ventilation)... and they soon became filled, from cellar to garret [attic], with a class of tenantry living from hand to mouth, loose in morals, improvident in habits, degraded or squalid as beggary itself.[2]

Did you notice the date of that quotation? It's 1857!

The quotation may seem to show prejudice against the people of the area, but it expresses what many have come to expect from a low income, tenant population (as distinguished from home owners).[3]

New construction in the area adapted to the new population's economic requirements. Houses were built much closer together. Large yards had additional houses built in them. Later, many duplexes and apartment buildings would go up, on the assumption that most of the people in the area would never be home owners.

But then transportation improved. Horse-drawn cars had traveled at a speed of three miles per hour. The new cable cars traveled fourteen miles per hour.[4] This made it possible for more people to live farther from downtown and still come in to work or do business.

Now more than ever, only the poor were left in the inner city.

A perhaps surprising development was that better transportation reduced the employment available downtown. It was no longer necessary for factories to be centrally located. Their supplies could be brought to them and their products sent out

---

2 Report of the Select Committee Appointed to Examine into the Condition of Tenant Houses in New York and Brooklyn," transmitted to the Legislature March 9, 1857 (Albany, NY) 11-12. Quoted by Banfield in *Heavenly City Revisited*, 27.

3 Other forms of prejudice are frowned on today, but prejudice against low income renters is assumed to be realistic, leading to such comments as, "There's no sense in fixing it up nice; they'll just tear it up." A landlord with such assumptions has abandoned any attempt to build a relationship of trust with tenants, and sees them as strangers paying for a temporary service. He would not dream of applying the "golden rule" to his renovation decisions.

4 Cable cars were introduced in Chicago in 1882.

13

more easily than before. Most factories were moved out of the center of the city to cheaper land.

It was also no longer as important for large retail businesses to be located downtown. Their stock and their customers could be brought to them.

Downtown no longer held the "monopoly of accessibility" as it did when it was the only place where a business or factory could thrive.

So what became of the downtown? Fewer jobs were available in the center. Office buildings and banks, businesses where many people need to work together, were still there, but those did not provide jobs for the uneducated and unskilled people in the inner city.

And what happened in the housing area that ringed the downtown, providing housing for workers? Now many of the residents were unemployed. The residential property ringing the downtown was no longer so valuable. Already it had been rented by lower-wage workers, but now there were not enough jobs to fill the area with employed workers.

The Great Depression began in 1929 and lasted at least a decade. This further lowered the number of jobs in the city, making the housing less valuable. More people left, looking for resources elsewhere.

The wartime economy (World War II, 1939-1945) flooded the inner city with workers again, but the prosperous continued to move out through the 40's.

Each new wave of immigrants flowed into the inner city because that was where housing was cheapest, but as families prospered they moved out.

Then came the great wave of immigration in the 1900's. It was not international, but was the migration of blacks from the South to the North. The South was mechanizing farming, eliminating workers; and the North was building factories, adding workers. Millions of blacks in the South were unemployed and decided to move north.

From 1915-1960, five million blacks moved north. Most bought the cheapest train tickets, which took them to the largest cities. Detroit went from a black population of 6,000 in 1910 to 120,000 by 1929.

> **From 1915-1960, five million blacks moved north.**

People in established communities felt invaded. Cities built project housing to supply the need for low income residences, and ghettoes (intentionally or not) were formed. The "projects" became known for violence, crime, poverty, vandalism, and hopelessness. There was a stigma attached to having to live in the "projects."

Northern blacks also resented the arrival of the southern blacks, who tended to be from rural backgrounds, less skilled, less educated, and generally less cultured than the northern blacks.

There already were not enough jobs, and the job supply continued to decrease as some factories moved south or overseas.

The blacks filled much of the inner city, as each wave of immigrants before them had done, because the cheapest space was there.

The term *white flight* has been coined to refer to the great exodus of the white population during this time. It is often assumed that the whites moved out because of foreign immigrants and blacks moving in. To some extent that is true, but prosperity was always a primary mover. People left because they could afford something better. But as the character of the inner city was changed by the departures, those who remained had further reasons to want out, and the departures began more and more to look like "flight."

The "flight" phenomenon did not begin with the black migration. It had started long ago due to economic trends. A committee of Boston citizens stated in the 1840's:

> An individual's influence is exerted chiefly in the place where he resides. Take away from the city a hundred moral and religious families, and there will be taken away a hundred centers of moral and religious influence, though the constituted heads of those families spend the greatest part of their time in the city, and hold in the metropolis the greatest proportion of their property [These are men who do business in the city but do not live there]. Those who remove their residence from the city remove also their places of attendance on public worship, and the children of those families are removed from our primary and higher schools...They are not here to visit the poor and degraded, and by their example and conduct to assist in resisting the tide of iniquity that is rolling in on us.[5]

White churches failed to engage.

The modern "flight" took on racial overtones because this time the millions of immigrants were not a different nationality but a different race.

White churches failed to engage. Subject to the same fears, prejudices, and lack of understanding of what was happening that everyone else had, the churches failed to rise to the occasion, welcome the newcomers, and build Christian community with them.

---

5 Quoted by J. Leslie Dunstan, *A Light to the City*, 91.

Once the situation grew more tense, it would have been even harder for the church to step in. The whites saw increase of crime and welfare dependency, just as they had feared. The blacks saw discrimination and intolerance, just as they had feared.

Ray Bakke and Jon Sharpe describe what they observed in Chicago:

These folks believed the Bible, but in a moment of panic they grabbed their Bibles and literally ran from the city. Good folks who believed and sponsored foreign missions ran from the city as foreigners moved into their neighborhoods. The Baptists took their evangelism and ran. The Pentecostals and charismatics took the Spirit and ran. The Reformed churches took their justification by faith and ran. The city became a religious ghost town. Even staff members from Moody, Trinity, and Wheaton fled the city.[6]

"Nothing prepared me for the cultural captivity and failure of my church under pressure."[7]

White flight was not a reaction merely to the black migration, but was a continuation of the processes that had already been forming what is called the "inner city." For a long time, those who could afford to leave the inner city had been doing so, leaving the poorest, which often included foreign immigrants.

As cities became more populous and culturally complex, white evangelical churches followed their members who had relocated outside the city. Between 1970 and 1980, Chicago lost one third of its white citizens; St. Louis lost 27%; Los Angeles lost 16%.[8]

The Federal Housing Authority (FHA) was created in 1934 to subsidize home building by insuring mortgages, mostly on

6 Ray Bakke and Jon Sharpe, *Street Signs,* 35.
7 Ray Bakke, *A Theology as Big as the City,* 21.
8 Keith Philips, *Out of Ashes,* 63, quoting Charles Gloab and Theodore Brown, *A History of Urban America,* 3rd ed., 384.

new homes. This meant that loans for home building would be made available to people who could not afford them before. However, the effect would not be to alleviate inner city conditions, but to worsen them. Vacant land for new homes was mostly available in the suburbs, which meant that an approved applicant from the inner city would be moving out. This again skimmed off the level of people in the inner city who were already doing better than most.

For an existing house to qualify for an FHA loan, it had to meet qualifications that excluded most inner city houses.

Racial segregation was written into FHA policy. Houses in areas with what the FHA Underwriting Manual called "inharmonious racial or nationality groups," areas with both blacks and whites, were required to be appraised low. That changed in 1962, when a presidential order barred discrimination in federally aided housing. Until then, few blacks could take advantage of the opportunity, since they would not be assisted to move into white or mixed areas, and few houses in black areas would qualify.

> **Racial segregation was written into FHA policy.**

The VA program was similar. Therefore, in effect, these programs assisted white workers to move out of the inner city into white areas, and denied funds for renovation of the inner city.

In 1968, the Fair Housing Act made it illegal for blacks to be discriminated against in buying houses in particular neighborhoods. More prosperous blacks immediately began to move out of the inner city, further concentrating poverty there. Black-owned businesses were often sold to foreign immigrants, as the children of black business owners chose not to stay in the inner city.

Housing programs over the years have contributed to rapid suburbanization and unplanned urban sprawl,[9] to growing residential separation of the races, and to the concentration of the poor and minorities in decaying central [inner] cities.[10]

Why does a community of poverty seem to inevitably have high crime, property deterioration, vandalism, and high family disfunction? It's not because poor people tend to have bad char acter; however, among those in the lowest economic class are those who are there because of bad character, and those tend to dominate the environment. For example, if 10% of the people in a community were violent and larcenous, the community would appear to have that character, though the generalization would be unfair to the other 90%.[11]

What happens when a society crams historically oppressed, uneducated, unemployed, and relatively young human beings into high-rise buildings, takes away their leaders, provides them with inferior education, health care, and employment systems, and then pays them not to work? Is it really surprising that we see out-of-wedlock pregnancies, broken families, violent crimes, and drug trafficking? Worse yet, we end up with nihilism, because these broken systems do serious damage to people's worldviews.[12]

---

9 "Urban sprawl" is the spread of a city over a wider area, usually turning farmland into residential areas, with the results that land around the city rises in price, city transportation systems are challenged, and many more people are using city services during the day than are paying city taxes.

10 *The President's Fourth Annual Report on National Housing Goals*, 92nd Congress, 2nd session, House Document No. 92-319, June 29, 1972. Quoted by Banfield in *Heavenly City Revisited*, 17.

11 Current trends mean that that the inner city is no longer unique in its conditions. There are many other neighborhoods in a large city that are like the inner city, especially if large apartment complexes of subsidized housing are built. There is even a present reversal of white flight, as professionals are returning to live in the city, and many of the poor are moving to the suburbs.

12 Steve Corbett and Brian Fikkert, *When Helping Hurts*, 92.

Chapter 3
The Inner-City Street Economy

Tasha called her pastor with exciting news of an answer to prayer. Part of making a new start in life had included moving to Indianapolis from another state. She lacked money to buy curtains and other things to fix up her new apartment, but then her food stamps came in, and she was able to sell them for the things she needed.

The inner city economy runs mostly on government money from social security, welfare, disability support, retailed food stamps, and prescription drugs resold to addicts.

After being in and out of jail for his violent reactions, and through many counseling sessions for his erratic behavior, Ben was labeled as unable to hold employment. He was approved to receive a monthly check for support, and was prescribed pills for emotional stability. To buy the narcotic he preferred, he supplemented his check by selling his pills, and visited area ministries for food.

Other government money comes into the local economy through Section 8 housing and child care assistance. Section 8 money docs not stay in the area, but does motivate the renovation and maintenance of houses there.

"You should get your house approved for Section 8 renters," Sharon advised the investor renovating the house next door. "That's what I get, and once a person gets approved for Section 8 to pay their rent, it goes on forever."

Much of the money spent in the inner city immediately leaves rather than circulating there. This problem is called "the escaping urban dollar." Most rented houses are owned by landlords outside the inner city. Businesses like gas stations, convenience stores, and fast food restaurants all take the money out. Services for the inner city funded by the government represent money that immediately is taken out, such as police, firemen, and social workers. Even grant money for rebuilding the inner city buys materials elsewhere and hires workers from elsewhere.

> **Much of the money spent in the inner city immediately leaves.**

The businesses that flourish in the inner city are pawn shops, liquor stores, tattoo parlors, and check cashers. Grocery stores struggle, but vending machines do well if protected.

Some households survive by combining people in various conditions. A household's income contributors may include a retiree or disabled person, a single mother on food stamps, a special needs child or adult on Social Security, and one or more adults who get occasional odd jobs. Each lives there on whatever terms he has worked out with whoever is in control of the house. Terms are not equal or constant, but fluctuate with circumstances and relationships.

A person with an income and no supporting relationships may rent a room by the week. Large houses are rented out by the room to an assortment of individuals who share the bathrooms and kitchens.

Many inner-city residents donate blood plasma frequently because they are paid for it.

"Scrapping" is the collection of scrap metal for recycling. Anything metal put out by the road will be picked up within a few minutes. An empty house with aluminum siding or gutters may be stripped. People without cars push grocery carts to take cans and other metal to the recycling plant, then abandon the carts. Recycling companies refuse to buy telephone wire, manhole covers, railroad material, or grocery carts.

Ed was furious when he went back to continue work at the house he was renovating. Someone had gotten into the house and taken out everything that was metal, including the furnace, the hot water heater, and even the vent covers in the floor. They had pulled the wiring out of the walls, ripping the new drywall. He had to reframe all of the vent openings, because the covers had been antique ones, of sizes difficult to find.

Relationships between landlords and renters are flexible. The landlord may overlook the dogs in the house, minor damage, and late payments. The renter endures substandard conditions such as lights or plumbing fixtures that don't work, leaking roofs, door jambs splintered from previous break-ins, cracked window panes, and poor drywall repair. Both know that to demand more would end the relationship. A tenant does not feel bound to stay for the term of his lease, but will move at any time, typically not paying for the last month of his stay. He will leave behind debris and unwanted household items.

Amber was crying as she stood on the icy sidewalk that winter evening. Her boyfriend needed money for another fix and had driven her out of the house to make some money any way possible. A church van stopped, and the pastor wanted to help her, but how could she explain her problem to him?

> **Prostitution is an established part of the inner-city economy.**

Prostitution is an established part of the inner-city economy. The woman may be a single mother stretching her income to get through the month, an addict trading sex for drugs, a homeless woman needing a place to stay, or even a girlfriend ordered out to raise some money. The price can be $20 or less.

"I told Amos he had to go back to Detroit and try to get some money." Angel was explaining why her boyfriend was gone again. She drew what government assistance she could for herself and her five children, but the cash didn't stretch to the end of the month. Amos was extra weight on the budget, and his presence also hindered Angel from her sideline of street-walking. She occasionally needed him out of the way so she could earn the extra money the family needed.

For decades, John Perkins has been a leader in responding to urban issues from the perspective of the black community. The quotation below addresses especially the conditions of black families, but applies to the population of the inner city in general:

> Before welfare, it took a two-parent family to survive. Now the single mother with children, helped by programs like Aid to Families with Dependent Children (AFDC), anchored the new economy of the inner city. Despite good intentions, AFDC has helped to forestall and break up more black families than anything since slavery's auction blocks sold husbands, wives, and children in different directions. Sadly enough, it also provides much of the revenue for the inner-city drug trade.[13]

---

[13] John Perkins, *Beyond Charity: The Call to Christian Community Development*, 10. Obviously one program is not solely responsible for inner-city conditions, nor does Perkins intend to imply that. However, the inner-city economy is funded primarily by various government programs.

Chapter 4
Where Time Is Forgotten

Orientation to the present is typical of cultures where people have little sense of control over future events. There may not be political freedom, financial resources, economic opportunities, and cultural individualism.

The individual is not conscious of being able to make decisions that affect his future; therefore, no habit of planning develops. No process of decision making is learned. He does not learn how to adapt behavior in the light of consequences.

Missionaries and other kinds of project directors get frustrated because the people of those cultures cannot seem to get motivated to make changes. It is also difficult to find individuals among them who can be hired and motivated to accomplish things, but it can be done, because in any culture, something of human nature responds to individual incentive and responsibility.

Present Orientation in Inner City Culture

Edward Banfield insightfully (though perhaps simplistically) diagnosed inner-city poverty and its aspects as a single problem:

> The lower-class forms of all problems are at bottom a single problem: the existence of an outlook and style of life which is radically present-oriented and which therefore attaches no value to work, sacrifice, self-improvement, or service to family, friends, or community.

Present orientation comes from a sense of powerlessness to affect future conditions, sometimes from a previous generation

24

that conditioned him to dependency, and from natural fallen desires that resist personal discipline. The description below is of the person most extreme in this tendency. There are many who have some of these characteristics to various degrees.

What matters to him is what he is experiencing right now.

If something is available that he wants, he will spend whatever he has to get it. Whatever money is in his pocket is to be used today. A certain form of generosity comes easily to him, because if he has more right now than he needs, he feels that he should share it with someone else. He will resent others who keep more than they need at the moment instead of sharing with him.

Nothing has any value to him except what he can use right now. If he has something valuable that he does not need today, he may convert it into cash to be spent today.[14]

> **Nothing has any value to him except what he can use right now.**

His grocery shopping is usually for snack food at a convenience store. He does not hesitate to pay a high price at the ice cream truck coming down the street. A family may spend their last money eating out at a fast food restaurant.

If he has a car, he usually buys five dollars' worth of gas, or less, at a time, because that will get him where he wants to go now, and he wants to spend the rest of his money on something else that he can enjoy today. He most likely will not have a car long, because he doesn't understand maintaining licensing and insurance or maintenance.

If he works, he wants to get paid the same day. If he were not going to get paid today, it would be hard for him to feel like

---

14 Edward Banfield, *The Unheavenly City Revisited*, 235.

it was worthwhile to work. That's why if he does get a regular job, he spends his paycheck in two or three days, and then he doesn't have a job, because he didn't see the need to go to work for that three days while he had money to spend.

This present-focused person is usually uneducated, because you don't get educated for the present; you get educated for the future. He doesn't have skills, because a skill is developed by training and practice, and that takes time before it gains you something.

His long-term health is not something he thinks about. He does want to feel better now. Pain will drive him to seek medical help, but otherwise he does not think about how his actions are affecting his health and shortening his life.

He will never own a house. If someone gave him a house, he would borrow money on it and spend it, then lose it by not making payments. If he were not allowed to borrow, he would live there until the house became uninhabitable for lack of repairs, then leave it and rent somewhere.

Decades will roll by with no change in his circumstances. When he is fifty years old, he will roam the streets and live exactly like he did when he was twenty, and have the same sense of responsibility that he had at fourteen.

Relationships and Interactions

The focus on the present affects child raising – consistent child discipline is difficult and pays off only over time, so instead there is indulgence part of the time and flashes of temper part of the time, and the child never knows which to expect. A child by age five learns that there are no guarantees that he can earn anything, and that no promises are kept, so begins to become the same kind of person (a person who assumes that his actions do not have predictable consequences).

He has little basis for self-esteem, but tries to maintain some dignity by choosing when to cooperate with others. He will carefully avoid any appearance of being compelled to do anything. He is sensitive to any treatment that seems to assume that he does not have options. Small symbolic actions of respect or disrespect are important to him.[15]

He never has a real marriage or family, because that takes commitment that has to last through days when there don't seem to be benefits.

The households are female-based. The series of men in the household take no responsibility for the children. A woman who is the mother or

> **The households are female-based.**

aunt or grandmother of the children in the household tries to provide some stability, but the odds are against her, and once the children are beyond babyhood, they are neglected or dealt with harshly.

Disadvantaged

He accumulates a lot of disadvantages. Success is the accumulation of advantages: education, skills, relationships, references, credit, and reputation. The person who is successful is the one who is able to respond to opportunity with advantage. Failure comes with the accumulation of disadvantages: no education, no skills, no relationships, no references, bad credit, and bad reputation. When a job opportunity comes along, he doesn't qualify for it.

---

15 This subject is dealt with more thoroughly in the chapter "Poverty and Dignity."

Sense of Powerlessness

Why does he not do what will have good results? Why doesn't he take action to improve his future?

He doesn't see a connection between present actions and future conditions. He does not see any connection between what he does and what happens to him. That's why he does not make plans and does not determine to accomplish anything. He takes each day as it comes.

He resents all authority and will ignore it when he can. Since he does not see the significance of his own actions, he does not understand why his actions matter to anyone else.

When he makes promises, they don't mean what they sound like. How can he make a promise when he has no control over the future? When he says he will do something in the future, he doesn't really mean he will make sure it happens; he is just agreeing with you that it would be a good thing to happen. When he fails to do what he said he would do, he hardly even feels the need to make an excuse. It just didn't happen.

If someone else has more than he has, he assumes they were just lucky. He doesn't see how their actions affect what they have. They are merely fortunate to have it, and he is unfortunate to be in need. Therefore, he assumes they should share it with him.

His story is full of interesting experiences, adventures, misfortunes, tragedies, losses, and injustices. The story is about things that have happened to him. It is not about what he has done. He does not make things happen; things happen to him. He does not see any connection between what he did and what happened to him. In his story, his actions are only responses to what happened to him, and every action is excusable under the circumstances.

Graffiti and Vandalism

The young male in the inner city is driven to act and choose in a world that is out of his control and under forces that try to control him. His attempt to assert himself may take the form of violence. Ironically even apathy and stubbornness may be assertion, so he can at least feel and demonstrate that he is not being compelled. He would rather fail a test than appear to be manipulated by the teacher's incentives and arguments. Consequences are less important than the sense of acting freely, the sense that he is a person that has to be accounted for. Lacking the models of heroism and the opportunities for it, he becomes a hero of a different kind, one who can be stubborn, cruel, or tough without fearing results. To act according to consequences could seem like coming under control. Men talk about the prison sentences they have served, to show that they did what they wanted without concern for consequences.

Graffiti is the attempt to express a message in a counter-cultural way, rebelling against the status quo. People have proposed that a prevention of graffiti would be for someone to make a white wall available for art. That idea misses the point of graffiti. It's not just art; it's art expressing rebellion. A wall freely provided would be no good for graffiti.

> **A wall freely provided would be no good for graffiti.**

Vandalism is a similar statement or act of striking back assertively. The young man cannot build anything or accomplish anything positive, but he can break something. It's the only way he has of making a mark on his environment. It's an adolescent form of nihilism.

29

Why People Are Present-Oriented

The problem is not because of low intelligence.

There are at least three kinds of people in the mix.

(1) Those who lapsed into the mindset after failure to achieve (deciding that incentives are meaningless)

(2) Those who dropped there from other environments because of weak character (they know better, but can't do it because of inner weakness)

These may have been successful home owners and business owners in the past, but came under the control of an addiction which consumed their resources and destroyed their credibility.

(3) Those who grew up in a present-oriented culture and know nothing else (conditioned to it from birth)

It is not so much that they have adapted to a life of blocked opportunities (because of poverty, discrimination, unavailable employment) in early adulthood, but that as infants and young children in the inner city they were assimilated into a present-oriented culture.

A study found that children who were highly deprived of parental interaction were unlikely to play at building something or projecting any sequence that involved making a plan and carrying it out. A child's ability to make a plan and carry it out may be connected to its mother's responses to its early efforts at play. If the mother interacts with the child's actions, he gains the sense of being able to make things happen. If she holds him passively and does not respond positively to him while feeding and cleaning, he does not have the feeling that he can make things happen. A deprived child at age three or four may still be at the sensory or motor level of play, without goals, or running around without purpose, (Banfield, 247-248).

There is something called a time horizon. A time horizon is (1) the point in the future beyond which nothing matters; that is, beyond which one cannot draw implications for present action, or (2) the point beyond which one cannot influence events. The present-oriented person may have a time horizon that hardly extends beyond today.

Time horizon can be extended by (1) new knowledge about circumstances, (2) acceptance of goals that are more distant in the future, (3) reduction of uncertainty about future possibilities, and (4) an increase in personal ability to influence the future.[16]

Why It Matters

To be human means that we are creatures in the image of God. God has put something of His nature in us. We will live forever, yet that timelessness does not mean we can go back and undo mistakes. We are creatures of eternity who make irrevocable choices.

> **We are creatures of eternity who make irrevocable choices.**

God created us to live in relationship with Him, guided by Him, and bringing glory to Him with our lives. Humanity has a destiny. You as a human have an individual destiny. But that destiny is not set to happen inevitably, no matter what you do. You are a creature in the image of God making decisions with eternal consequences.

Why would anyone give that up?

There is a weakness of character in fallen human nature. This weakness brings the temptation to surrender the human

---

16 Adapted from Banfield, 239-240.

destiny, to accept helplessness as an excuse for doing what is easy and taking what is available now.

But to do that is not only to reject God, it is to reject yourself. It is to reject the status of being human that God created you for.

How Can We Help People Learn to Live with an Eternal Focus?

In God's Word, a certain kind of person is called a sluggard. He is idle because he is not motivated by hope and purpose. He is to look at the example of the ant, which shows foresight and initiative without compulsion, rather than focus on the present.

Life has a natural tendency to teach the concept of consequences. That's why not everything that is intended to help people really helps. Social programs that help without incentive actually hinder learning, because they undermine the natural teaching of life.

The church has a message of hope, based on God's power, to the person who has lived apart from God and has a will weakened by many wrong choices. The message has to come through people that earn trust. The present-conditioned person needs guarantees from people he trusts in order to put forth effort.

God responds to the blind with vision and light. He responds with hope for the hopeless – not hope in self, but hope in God when self is made available for Him. He responds with power on the inside for the one with weak character. He accomplishes transformation and anointing by the Spirit power.

And He creates a community of faith with new relationships of trust and care.

Chapter 5
It's Not the Money

The condition of the American inner-city poor is not just poverty due to a lack of resources. If that were the essential problem, it would already have been solved by the resources that have been poured into the inner city.

Types of Government Assistance Available

TANF (Temporary cash assistance for needy families)

Section 8 Housing

Medical Care

Monthly Welfare Checks

Food Assistance (SNAP: Supplemental Nutrition Assistance Program)

WIC (Food given for women, infants, and children)

Disability Benefits

School Breakfast and Lunch

Unemployment Benefits

College Scholarships

Child Care (which leads to the licensing of approved day cares)

Child Education

Transportation to Medical Appointments

Cell Phones

Typical Assistance from Churches

Served Meals

Pantries

School Supplies

Types of Assistance from Organizations Secular or Religious

Medical Clinics

Addiction Recovery Programs

Job Skill Training

Resume Writing and Job Search Assistance

High School Education Completion or GED Tutoring

Some Specific Dollar Amounts for a Single Month[17]

$25,570,974 in food assistance was issued in February 2014, in Marion County, Indiana, to 93,394 households.

$4,776,736 in child care was paid in February 2014, in Marion County, Indiana, for 12,205 children.

Measuring Program Effectiveness

How should the success of poverty alleviation efforts be measured? Many measurements have been used.

By apparent gratitude? (Assumption: Immediate responses of the recipient are sufficient indicators.)

By attraction of clients? (Assumption: If they didn't really need it they wouldn't come for it.)

By the amount spent? (Assumption: More spent means more accomplished.)

---

17 Reported on Indiana state website:
http://www.in.gov/fssa/files/counties.

By the number of people helped? (Assumption: More people need to be helped.)

By program efficiency? (Assumption: We should give the most help possible for the price.)

By increased funding? (Assumption: The program should grow like a successful business does.)

The best measurement is the percentage of people helped who become less dependent.[18] Help should enable a change of circumstances rather than survival in unchanged circumstances. The best thing you can offer a person in poverty is the opportunity to change his situation.

> **The best thing you can offer a person in poverty is the opportunity to change his situation.**

This meets the real need instead of using people for an agenda. It may have the effect of reducing some of the numbers produced by the other kinds of measurements listed above. For example, an effective job training program will lower the number of people needing some kinds of assistance, could lower the amount spent on other programs, and will attract fewer "clients" than an easy giveaway.

The more effective a program is, the more obsolete it is to the people it has already served.[19]

---

18 Different standards would apply to programs for people who are unable to be independent because of physical or mental limitations.

19 That means that a church based only on an effective intervention program will not keep the people it helps, because it will become irrelevant to them. To build a congregation, the church must be a community of faith that gains the commitment of the people served.

Measuring Present Effectiveness of Government Assistance[20]

The following statistics are for federal food assistance in the United States.

1980   21 million recipients   cost: $9,000,000,000

1990   20 million recipients   cost: $15,000,000,000

2000   17 million recipients   cost: $17,000,000,000

2010   40 million recipients   cost: $68,000,000,000

The last decade showed a doubling of the number of recipients and a tripling of the cost. That trend is continuing, as shown by the 2013 figures, coming not a decade later, but only three years later.

2013   48 million recipients   cost: $80,000,000,000

Who would consider this program successful? Maybe the person who thinks many needy people are being neglected would be glad to see the program grow. People who direct the program might be glad to see it grow. Politicians who build a constituency of people supported by the government are glad to see the numbers grow.

Attempts at Accountability

Institutions that try to alleviate poverty soon become concerned about the misuse of their giving. Resources given to meet a specified need may get used for some other purpose by the recipient. The problem is that the recipients see the purposes of the institution as irrelevant to their needs and usually don't coop-

---

20 From U.S. government website: :
http://www.fns.usda.gov/pd/SNAPsummary.htm Numbers of recipients are rounded to the nearest million, and cost amounts are rounded to the nearest billion.

erate with those purposes. The institution is trying to accomplish something for the recipient that the recipient is not interested in.

To accomplish their purposes, institutions implement policies that put terms on their giving.

Institutional policies try to...

(1) Make sure the assistance goes to its intended use ("This can be spent only for food.")

(2) Prevent overuse of the services ("You can come once a week.")

(3) Use the assistance as leverage to serve an unrelated purpose ("To get this money, you have to fill out three job applications somewhere.")

(4) Make sure the recipients are truly needy ("Bring proof that you are not employed.")

"The Game" is what results as institutions try to enforce the proper use of their gift, and recipients find ways to receive money for their own purposes.

It is assumed that cash given to the needy will probably be misused, so programs try to meet specific needs in a way that limits the options of the recipient. Food stamps can be spent at stores only for food. WIC goes even farther, selecting what food to give.

> **"The Game" is what results as institutions try to enforce the proper use of their gift.**

In spite of these precautions, there is a flourishing market for food stamps to be traded for cash. People regularly drop off both food stamp cards and cash cards to local drug dealers or make bargains with their neighbors.

Pantries require identification so they can limit how often a person comes. A church that gives away food after their service may require that recipients be there before service to get a food ticket.

To receive TANF, a person is supposed to be trying to get a job. That is verified by requiring him to turn in a certain number of job applications. There is no way to make sure he is really making the effort necessary to get hired.

To make sure that recipients are truly needy, interviewers ask them about their income, property, and help from others. If the applicant confesses that he has earned any wages, his assistance is reduced. The response of the case worker will imply that wage earning is a wrong doing that must be penalized. The more irresponsible the applicant has been, the more assistance he will qualify for. If he reports that he earned some cash, which would otherwise have been undetectable, he will be required to prove the amount, which may be impossible. He knows he is better off not to confess any income.

Is there a way to avoid "the game" entirely? Maybe not completely, but a genuine personal relationship based on openness and driven by spiritual priorities helps to make many of the subterfuges irrelevant. There is a difference between service organizations (inside or outside the church) and a church that is in true community. The church is uniquely equipped by God to respond to the real need.

Part 2:

The Church

Chapter 6
More than a Glance

As Yogi Berra supposedly said, "It's amazing how much you can observe just by looking around." Just taking a scenic drive through the heart of the city you will notice that there are already many people involved in alleviating the problems of the inner city. Upon first sight of poverty conditions, you may exclaim, "Why doesn't somebody do something?" But a lot of things are being done by a lot of people.

One might assume that the sheer size of the need means that the solution will involve getting more and more people to come to the place of need, bringing labor and energy for rebuilding, and giving resources to the impoverished.

In the United States, the government pours millions of dollars into every major city every month, providing food stamps, welfare, subsidized housing, child care, medical care, and disability support. Various organizations, some government supported, get into the act with drug recovery programs, counseling, job training, GED programs, resume writing, and home renovation.

Churches and parachurch ministries provide services to the poor such as homeless shelters, soup kitchens, and pantries.

A person who spends time helping at one of these ministries soon realizes that he is serving people who have been in the same condition for many years. Looking at the neighborhood, he realizes that many problems seem untouched, though organizations have poured in resources for many years.

So here is the pressing question: Why haven't the efforts of alleviation made greater changes in the areas of poverty?

To begin to answer that question takes more than a glance. We have to ask questions and be ready to listen with discernment.

Another thing you soon notice as you get beyond a glance is that among those involved in alleviating conditions of poverty are very different beliefs about what the real needs are.

The variety of approaches to poverty alleviation comes from different perceptions of what the problem is and what the solution is.

If the problem is a lack of resources, redistribution of resources is a solution, and the big issue is whether that should happen by taxation or other means.

If it's crime (as in the unrestrained behavior of a few), law enforcement or neighborhood organizing is the solution.

If it's ignorance (as in people not knowing how to do better), information and training are the solution.

If it's lack of opportunity (as in some people lacking access to the means of progress), subsidized opportunities reserved for selected categories of people are the solution.

If it's discrimination (as in the unjust restriction of opportunities), require equal opportunity.

If it is sin, the gospel is the solution. Evangelicals believe that the gospel is the first and comprehensive answer to human problems, but that still does not make all the issues simple.

Evangelicals, who believe that sin is the primary problem and that the gospel is the primary solution, must go on to consider questions like these.

Since eternal destiny is the greatest issue, how much time and resources should be spent on ministering to needs other than spiritual ones?

What does the gospel encompass?

What does the gospel encompass? Is the good news only the message of God's forgiveness? What differences are made by the "gospel of the kingdom" for life in this world?

How much does the church's mission include a compassionate response to practical needs and societal conditions?

How is a local church, with apparently limited resources, yet identified in Scripture as the local body of Christ living in the abundance of the kingdom of God, supposed to respond to the needs of all kinds that surround it?

How far should ministry go toward meeting needs that are sin based? How much help should we give to an unrepentant person whose problems are because of ongoing sin?

One principle is that we should not provide help that merely relieves an unrepentant sinner of the consequences of his sin while he continues in it. But some situations are complicated because people are suffering from the ongoing actions of other people.

For example, should we help feed the children of a drug addict, knowing that our help may make the addict feel even less responsibility? Should we give food and other resources to a household where the children are neglected because the adults are unwilling to work? Should we provide clean needles and condoms for people that are "going to do it anyway" to try to prevent the spread of disease?

To develop a philosophy of ministry in conditions of poverty, we need to ask questions of the right people, analyze the differences between their answers, observe first-hand, evaluate by God's truth, pray for understanding, learn from history, and practice Christian faith in the real-world laboratory.

Chapter 7
Why It Matters to the Church

The mission of the church is to continue the ministry of Jesus in the world.[21] So why did Jesus come? He stated His mission in Luke 4:18-19:

"The Spirit of the Lord is upon me, because he has anointed me to preach the gospel to the poor; he has sent me to heal the brokenhearted, to preach deliverance to the captives, and recovering of sight to the blind, to set at liberty them that are bruised, to preach the acceptable year of the Lord."

This statement could be used to answer the question, "Why did Jesus come?" because Jesus said it is what He was anointed to do. It was the purpose predicted of Him in the Old Testament. That is not to say that it includes every aspect of His purpose, but we have to take seriously His own statement.

> **Sometimes churches see their ministry as exclusively spiritual.**

The first thing He said He was to do was to preach the good news to the poor. Since the church is the "body of Christ" in the world, His mission is the church's mission. The church can never claim to be fulfilling its mission if it neglects or excludes the poor.

Sometimes churches see their ministry as exclusively spiritual, but Jesus' description of His ministry shows that He expected to change earthly conditions. The "good news" He announced was not just the means of spiritual conversion; it

---

21 As the Father has sent me, so send I you" (John 20:21). "Whoever believes on me will do the works that I do" (John 14:12). "Now ye [the church] are the body of Christ" (1 Corinthians 12:27).

was the news that a new way of life in the Kingdom of God had begun.

Jesus said that the greatest command is to love your neighbor as yourself, and He gave the story of the Good Samaritan as an example. It was not an example of someone sharing the message of the gospel, but someone responding to a practical need.

Centuries before, the prophet Micah considered the question of what God really wants from His worshippers. He wondered whether herds of cattle, or a river of oil, or even a human child would be enough of a sacrifice. He then explained that it's not a matter of finding a sacrifice that is great enough to be worthy of God. God has revealed His expectations of us.

"He has shown you, O man, what is good, and what does the Lord require of you, but to do justly, and to love mercy, and to walk humbly with your God" (Micah 6:8).

We are responsible to do justice and try to help others receive justice. Mercy does not refer only to the kind use of authority. "Mercy" refers to the relief of needs. Jesus said that the Good Samaritan was an example of the love God commands because he "showed mercy."

Many local churches have assumed that issues of poverty are outside of their proper domain and that they should be dealing with spiritual issues only. Many pastors are prepared to answer doctrinal questions or tell someone what the Bible commands, but they consider material needs to be irrelevant to their ministry. Surely churches should be models of love on the pattern of the Good Samaritan.

Some Evangelicals reject social action and poverty relief as being less important than gospel proclamation. In their minds, because a dollar spent on poverty relief is a dollar that cannot be spent for the spread of the gospel, the right choice is obvious. However, they show their personal priorities by living where conditions are better instead of where the gospel is most needed. If they lacked food, or housing, or quality education for their children; or if they lived in a dangerous environment, those problems would immediately get their focus. So, ironically, what they say is most important for people in bad neighborhoods is that they hear the gospel, but what is most important for themselves is that they live in a better neighborhood.

The Bible mentions the poor about 400 times.	The Bible mentions the poor about 400 times.
	The city of Sodom is most remembered for the sin of sexual perversion, but the wickedness of the city, as God described it, was not that alone.

"Behold, this was the iniquity of your sister Sodom, pride, fullness of bread, and abundance of idleness was in her and in her daughters, neither did she strengthen the hand of the poor and needy. And they were haughty and committed abomination before me: therefore, I took them away as I saw good" (Ezekiel 16:49-50).

The sin of sexual perversion is perhaps the "abomination" mentioned in these verses, but social issues are emphasized first. They used their prosperity to provide leisure for themselves and did not find a way to empower the poor ("strengthen the hand") to change their situation.

Evangelicals do well to take a stand for sexual morality, but tend to avoid the other issues emphasized here.

Jeremiah wrote to Jews in captivity telling them what their relationship should be with the pagan society they were in. If any believers in God ever had reason to abstain from participation in society, surely these Jews did. They were there against their will; the religion of the society was pagan; the government was oppressive and had destroyed their nation, and they were waiting for the day when they could leave.

But listen to the message God gave the prophet for these people:

"Seek the peace [*shalom*] of the city where I have sent you into exile, and pray to the Lord on its behalf, for in its peace you will find your peace" (Jeremiah 29:7). *Shalom*, the word usually translated peace, refers not only to peace itself, but the blessings that accompany peace. It refers to the blessings of God. These worshippers of God exiled in a pagan country would find God's blessings as they tried to bring those blessings into a society that knew nothing of Him and had persecuted His people!

This certainly forbids the kind of separation from the world that implies unconcern about all except spiritual issues.

We know that what is wrong with our world is that individuals and organized powers do not regard God's Word. From God's revealed truth should come ethics (distinction between right and wrong), from ethics should come politics (principles of justice and freedom applied in society), and then economics (the use of all material resources).

The natural tendency of human society is to reverse that order. People make their personal economics the priority, then support leaders and laws that will give them what they want even at the expense of justice and freedom, then form their ethical systems to match what they do, then design religion to commend their behavior.

The church should stand for biblical truth, not only by denouncing the sins of society, but by explaining and demonstrating what society should be like. If we are so disconnected from society that we cannot explain and demonstrate what society should be doing, we can hardly be surprised if those who are more ignorant of biblical truth fail to apply it.

The reality is that even church members, who must live in the world and engage in its concerns, have not been taught what it means to live as citizens of the kingdom of God in daily life.

The church is often called the family of God, and members call each other brother and sister. We sing songs about the kinship felt by believers.

The family is a popular metaphor. Many companies call themselves families, but an employee is not actually in the company family because of the value of the relationship, but for other reasons. If an employee becomes unproductive he will be expelled from the family, and if the company ceases to pay him, he will leave the family and look for another.

Let's imagine the family as it has been understood in most parts of the world until modern times. The extended family provided protection, access to justice, land possession, employability, marriageability, education, old age support, orphan support, and widow support. Imagine a world where all of those things are hardly available outside of family connections.

> **The church became their family.**

Was this the kind of extended family that the converts to the early church entered? After all, it would have been the concept of the family that the people of most cultures held in the first century. Consider further that many converts to Christianity were alienated from their own families by their conversion. The church became their family in a fuller sense than we can imagine.

In the New Testament we see practical instructions to communities of believers sharing life as families. One passage especially gives us a glimpse of the responsibility the church felt for care of its members. There were people who were roaming around gossiping and doing nothing productive, yet depending on the church's support. Paul directed that people not be fed if they were not willing to work. This tells us that the church had developed an economy for the community of faith that made sure all members were supported and could also provide productive work for all.

According to the book of Ephesians, the church is called to be the body of Christ, the fullness of God in a place. That means that most of the blessings God wants to give to a community will come through the church. Those blessings should come in a way that takes care of people who are in relationship with God and His people, and outsiders should be continually invited to enter the family.

Now let's suppose that there is a congregation of believers in a poor community. A wealthy church in another place becomes aware of the poverty of the community and wants to help. What is the best way they can help? What usually happens is that representatives of the wealthy come and decide what is needed and by whom, and distribute resources.

That kind of giving bypasses and undermines the efforts of the church. The church already knows who is in the community. They know who is willing to work. They know what people are doing with the resources they already have. They know who has been offered opportunities already. The outsiders know none of that, but with their giving they make the work of the church irrelevant. Their giving is also completely unrelated to bringing people into relationship with God and the local group of God's people.

It would be better for the givers to talk to the congregation until they share the same vision of how God wants to bless the community, then let that blessing come through the church.

A biblical view of the mission of the church, the breadth of the gospel, and the community of faith will bring the church to confront all issues of poverty.

Chapter 8
Evangelicals and the Social Gospel

In every age, the church has the responsibility to speak to the conditions in society.

We repeat here a paragraph from a previous chapter.

The church should stand for biblical truth, not only by denouncing the sins of society, but by explaining and demonstrating what society should be like. If we are so disconnected from society that we cannot explain and demonstrate what society should be doing, we can hardly be surprised if those who are more ignorant of biblical truth fail to apply it.

In the mid 1900's, the responses of most churches and Christian leaders to the ills of society could be divided into two opposite categories. Among those who made statements about what the church should be doing, evangelical churches and liberal churches widely differed.

The Social Gospel

Liberal churches were the ones who had already taken the modernist direction in the modernist/fundamentalist debates of the previous decades. They had denied the inerrancy of Scripture and such fundamentals as the deity of Christ. They no longer had a scriptural gospel of salvation and transformation by grace.

Liberal churches taught Christianity primarily as an improved lifestyle. They believed that even if Jesus were just a man, His teachings are good directions for life. The supernatural was neglected if not denied. Eternal destiny was almost irrelevant, and life on earth was the focus.

Sin issues and eternal values were ignored. The immediate practical effect of beliefs was all that mattered. People who preached for salvation from sin were resented for not accepting people and for having misplaced concern about eternity instead of the here and now. As a tour guide at the Friend's Church in Philadelphia said, "If people would quit worrying so much about heaven, they might get more concerned about improving things on earth."

The liberals saw human nature as basically good and determined by environment. Like Dickens in *A Christmas Carol,* they saw the poor as primarily disadvantaged. The crime and abuses in the ghetto came from environment. They thought that by meeting material needs and changing the environment they would change the situation of the poor.

Many liberal churches took no interest in the issues of poverty, but those who did get involved applied the social gospel. They put into action their belief that Christianity provided directions for improving society and personal living. The spiritual side of Christianity was valued only for its practical usefulness in improving life, such as bringing comfort to the grieving.

> **Ultimately the social gospel fails, even in its earth-focused goals.**

Liberal churches started and funded hospitals, orphanages, and food distribution centers both in U.S. urban areas and in other countries.

Ultimately the social gospel fails, even in its earth-focused goals, for its proponents are not prepared to deal with fallen human nature. It fails to predict and avoid the dependency its policies create, assuming that the needy person will do his best to live a better life if he has the necessary resources. In many forms, it is unprepared to maintain accountability, underestimating the need for it. In more experienced forms, it tries to institute systems of accountability but cannot keep up with the subterfuges of recipients.

The liberal social gospel ignored basic Christian truth and lacked the advantage that Christians should have in such work:

> Christians living and working in cities can understand things that remain largely a mystery to persons lacking the biblical framework. Christians are very realistic about the city's essential nature and the cause of the unending frustrations that occur when citizens try to improve city life. Christians understand the root of the problem. It is the moral malignancy that lies buried deep in the city's heart. It is the legacy of Cain and the spirit of Lamech, which have never gone away."[22]

Evangelical Disengagement

Not all who claim to be evangelicals would agree on the same definition, but they tend to share certain characteristics. Evangelicals believe in the supreme authority of the Bible, the gospel of salvation by grace through faith, individual eternal destiny of heaven or hell, and a moment of conversion when a person experiences God's forgiveness and comes into relationship with God.

Evangelicals predicted and watched the failure of the social gospel of the liberals. Because the gospel was not the first concern, or even a concern at all, of the social programs, they knew that the cures of the social gospel were superficial.

---

22 Roger Greenway and Timothy Monsma, *Cities: Missions' New Frontier*, 30.

They saw some conservative Christian organizations that tried to do social work as a means of spreading the gospel turn into merely social organizations. Soup kitchens and dental clinics that were intended to provide contexts for presenting the gospel took on agendas of their own, and the gospel was crowded out. Those observations were used by evangelicals as evidence that social work was not a proper concern of the church.

This distancing of evangelicals from the ministry of poverty alleviation in 1900-1930 was a change from their earlier tradition, so much so that it has been called the "Great Reversal" by historians.[23] Earlier evangelical reformers and revivalists had been on the front lines of societal reform in England and America.

Evangelicals explained their detachment from social issues theologically on the basis of the gospel's priority. They considered gospel preaching, with its eternal results, to be of so much more value than meeting temporal needs that it would be poor stewardship to direct any funds or efforts away from gospel preaching toward social work.

Evangelicals saw the gospel as having primarily individual, spiritual application. They did not see the gospel of the kingdom as a message of a total way of life. The kingdom was spiritual and focused on heaven.

They believed that spiritual conversion is the real solution to an individual's problems, and that society's problems would not be solved until the return of Christ.[24]

If a ship is sinking, it is useless to arrange the chairs on the deck. It is better to try to save the passengers. This was common reasoning of those who considered it pointless to try to improve

23 George Marsden, *Fundamentalism and American Culture.*
24 This was also a departure from earlier evangelical reformers, who believed that their efforts would help Christianize the world and bring in the reign of Christ.

the living conditions of people rather than trying to get them converted.[25]

Since the purpose of the church is to get people converted and disciple them in the faith, social work is at best a means of getting people's attention for the gospel, and at worst a distraction from the real purpose of the church.

> **If a ship is sinking, it is useless to arrange the chairs on the deck.**

Evangelicals concentrated on personal evangelism, church growth, and foreign missions. The focus was bringing individuals to conversion. Critiques of American society tended to be condemnation of specific practices. The individual Christian was expected to stay separate from any structures where he could not live by Christian ethics; otherwise, no solutions were offered. Even less was there any overall program of addressing social evils (such as totalitarianism, racial conflicts, labor- management tensions, or international conflicts) with the goal of reforming them.

Evangelicals have tended to assume that conversion would give an individual the Christian perspective on social issues. However, many Christians involved in business, politics, or education do not well apply Christian principles, because they have not been taught how a Christian should approach the structures of the world. Therefore, conversion of more people without a "social" gospel may make little difference in structural evil.

---

25 However, if a Christian's living conditions were substandard, that would become his own focus until the problem was corrected. It should also be a focus if a brother is in need. If there were no such brothers in need, maybe the problem was failure to evangelize certain segments of society, in spite of the alleged priority of evangelism.

Evangelicals saw the church as a community mostly in spiritual matters. They did not develop a sense of economic community. As Americans in the land of opportunity, they accepted the individualism of the culture, assuming that anyone can make it if he tries, and that material help from the faith community should be limited to rare emergency situations. They assumed that opportunities for success are equally available to all.

Most evangelicals did not participate in civil rights work or reform.

Therefore, most evangelicals did not participate in civil rights work or reform. This was a departure from their own roots of revivalism and social reform.

Evangelicals lost touch with the culture of the inner city. They tended to despise the urban poor on moral grounds.

One result of the evangelical disengagement is that most evangelicals failed to develop a philosophy of ministry for contexts of poverty. Those who enter those contexts experiment in a variety of ways and repeat one another's mistakes. This happens both in the inner city and in foreign settings.

The Need for an Evangelical Social Gospel

Jesus quoted Messianic prophecies that described deliverance of the oppressed and various social reforms as His purpose for coming (Isaiah 58 and 61, quoted in Luke 4:16-21).

The biblical gospel confronts the individual with his need for repentance and reconciliation to God, but also describes a new way of life in the kingdom of God, which has begun on earth already.

A strength of the social gospel was that it tried to express the impact of the gospel on society and not just personal spirituality. Its failure was not because it had concern about the here and now, but because it did not approach social issues with a biblical understanding of sin, human nature, grace, and eternal destiny.

There is a biblical case for the gospel as a message that impacts social structures. Detachment from social issues eventually undermines even individual responsibility. A Christian feels justified working for a business that requires unbiblical practices of him, because he thinks he is not the one making the decisions.

There is also the corporate application of the gospel to the community of faith, so that Christians see themselves acting as a church and not just as individuals.

The social gospel was liberalized all the more because of abandonment by the evangelicals. It could be powerful when balanced and fueled by the evangelical message.

Chapter 9
Program or Gospel First?

A church served a meal for the community every Sunday afternoon for many years. Other churches in the area helped by bringing in meals and serving the food. Often a hundred or more people would gather to eat, many of them regulars. A few became helpful volunteers, setting up chairs, etc., but rarely attended a church service. The visiting church people who brought the food usually stayed behind the serving table or in the kitchen and did not sit at the tables. The pastor considered putting a brief devotional at the beginning of the meal, but never did, because he knew it would not be well accepted by those coming for the meal.

Christians agree that a person's spiritual need and eternal destiny are more important than his material needs. That doesn't mean that material needs don't matter to the church. The church is a community of faith, and all of a Christian's needs should be met through his participation in the life of the community. The epistle of James tells us that a lack of essentials such as food and clothing is not to be ignored by fellow believers. Needs should be met by the natural interactions that occur in the context of a relationship with God and His people.

When the church ministers to those who are outside the community of faith, the goal is to draw them into the relationship with God and His people. A church with a spiritual and eternal focus is not satisfied just to meet material needs and not spiritual ones. That is a difference between the church and most secular organizations that try to alleviate poverty.

However, the church has often struggled with the use of poverty relief programs to bring people into relationship with God. The theory of the "felt need" approach is that if you respond to the need a person feels, you begin a relationship, and he will believe that you care. You can then address the spiritual need in the context of that relationship. The assumption is that people do not respond to the gospel while worried about material problems, and that if a person tries to share the gospel without first helping in a practical way, his message will be ignored.

On those assumptions, a church may develop programs to respond to the needs of the neighborhood. The formula of this approach is program, then relationship, then gospel. The method could also be called the "program first" approach.[26]

Based on that theory, many ministries offer programs that respond to felt needs. They serve the needs of a neighborhood or target group, as far as resources allow. The goal is to create opportunities to share the gospel.

Unfortunately, there are many ways for programs of services to go wrong.

> **There are many ways for programs of services to go wrong.**

Sometimes service is provided without any relationship developing. Just as a person does not usually have lunch with his doctor, mailman, bank teller, or landlord, he may assume that his relationship to the ministry personnel will be limited to the service transaction. Ironically, the more efficiently the

---

26 The title may imply that the two approaches described here are opposites with nothing in common. In reality, various blending of these approaches do exist. The purpose of this chapter is especially to show that there is an approach that is more essential to the purpose of the church than the "program first" approach.

program is operated, the more likely it is that this will happen. The relationship may even be "one-way," where the recipient is confined to his role of neediness, with implied inferiority.

Giving through an institution becomes impersonal. When a person behind a desk approves you to receive something from the account he manages, that is not at all the same as when a brother or friend reaches into his pocket to help you with a need. When a friend helps, you are appreciative, you try not to take undue advantage, and you hope for a chance to help him. In contrast, the person behind the desk is thanked the same way a clerk is thanked for ringing up your purchase. It is very possible for a program to hinder the functioning of real Christian fellowship and charity.

Even if the program is started for the purpose of causing opportunities for sharing the gospel, it takes on a life of its own. Those responsible for food preparation, medical care, job training, or other service soon become focused on providing the service well and rarely have time for the kind of conversation that creates an opening for the gospel. A person may be appointed to serve as a kind of "chaplain," but he finds that he has to be creative to bring a spiritual focus into the swirl of activity. The gospel can seem to be artificially attached to what is going on and be easily ignored.

Since the gospel is not what is offered at the beginning, a "client base" is built up of people who have no interest in the gospel. The volunteer helpers from among the "clients" help with the program operation without even understanding its spiritual concern.

Conservation of resources soon becomes a concern and results in an ongoing contest between the recipients who want to get as much as they can and the staff who keep revising distribution policies to keep from running out. Recipients take as much as they can for as long as they can, then take their "business" elsewhere.

Ironically, the recipients may consider the program a success while the ministry seems to be failing in its purpose. It continually meets practical needs for them. They have no concern about the sidetracking of the church's purpose. They like best the very characteristics of the program that discourage the ministry staff.

Programs encourage the assumption that the church is there "to help people." Whenever a request is turned down either because of limited resources or because of unmet requirements, the objection is made, "Isn't the church supposed to help people?"

> **Programs encourage the assumption that the church is there "to help people."**

What if we turned the formula around? The formula should be gospel, then relationship, then help (and not necessarily help in the form of a program). Keep in mind that the gospel is not just the prescription for spiritual conversion, but also the good news of a present, redeemed life in the kingdom of God.

With this formula, the church sees its primary mission to be communicating the gospel, so it works at that constantly. As people respond to the message with interest, a relationship is formed. Whether the respondent is converted or not, he is at least attracted, interested, and intrigued by this group of people and their message.

Then, because he is in relationship with them (maybe not yet Christian fellowship, but relationship based on interest in the gospel lifestyle), whenever he has a need, they help him in practical ways. They help him find work; they share food if he is willing to work with them on projects, and they share their lives with him.

They may never develop programs for those things, such as a food pantry or an employment center. If they ever do, they risk becoming busy at providing those services for people who never came in through the relationship created by gospel ministry.

Part 3:

A Principled Approach

Chapter 10
Poverty and Dignity

A pastor was helping a family move. The family was father-less, consisting of a mother with several children, including a teenaged boy named Wallace. The pastor brought a truck belonging to the church and did the driving himself. He also helped with the loading and unloading. With a busy schedule, he hoped everything would go efficiently. He hurried back and forth between the house and the truck, carrying household goods, but quickly realized that something was wrong with Wallace. While the mother was friendly, grateful, and energetic, Wallace was silent and sluggish. He seemed to make a point of being unfriendly and unappreciative. He moved slowly and carried little, while the pastor, eager to finish, worked swiftly. Another oddity was that sometimes Wallace carried things that would normally require two people. He would take a large piece of furniture and struggle out to the truck with it, refusing help. The pastor was irritated and regretted getting himself into the situation.

It wasn't until later that the pastor realized what was going on. This family had moved often, and Wallace had always been the "man" in charge, trying to take care of the family. He resented the pastor's usurpation of his role. He did not want to help in a subordinate role, thus his sluggishness, and therefore he could not be cheerful about the situation. He did want to demonstrate that he could have handled the challenge without help; hence his effort with the large items.

If the pastor, upon arrival, had greeted Wallace as a key participant and had acknowledged him as nominally in charge by asking his opinion about some things, Wallace would have exerted more effort and would have been open to suggestions.

Dignity as a Neglected Value

We assume that people in need care only about getting help or resources, and we forget their need for dignity. We assume that dignity has been suspended under the circumstances. We may assume that they have already thrown away dignity by the way they ask. The "nerve" that people show in making some requests might even make us think they have no pride (like some people who stopped by a wedding reception to ask if they could take some food).

But often the poor are all the more sensitive to anything that seems like disrespect. They are without many of the symbols of security and success that could allow them to relax with a sense of secure status. They have long endured humiliating circumstances by having to ask for help that people in "normal" circumstances don't need (like food assistance), being unable to provide for their children things that other children have (like school uniforms or field trip money), and by having their poverty exposed at times of shortfalls (like having utilities disconnected). They therefore appreciate being treated with respect and are offended at anything that looks like a disregard of courtesy.

A pastor was picking up children for church. At one house, as he stood at the door, the child came and opened the door, then ran back to get her shoes. The mother came from another room and saw the pastor standing there holding the open door. She began to scold him because she thought he had opened the door. To her it seemed that he had not respected her house enough to knock and wait for the door to be opened. When he explained, she was satisfied.

An Old Testament law forbade creditors to enter the house of a debtor to take from him something that was used for loan collateral. A creditor was supposed to let the indebted person bring the collateral outside and give it to him. Imagine how impoverished a person feels if creditors can come boldly into his house, and in the presence of his family carry out the refrigerator while he is helpless to stop them.

"Poor people typically talk in terms of shame, inferiority, powerlessness, humiliation, fear, hopelessness, depression, social isolation, and voicelessness. North American audiences tend to emphasize a lack of material things such as food, money, clean water, medicine, housing, etc."[27] That may partly be because we have not experienced the indignity of lacking those things. This leads to efforts to alleviate poverty that ignore an essential human need.

Actions of Disdain

Some people tend to despise the poor if they ask for things. They say things like, "They just want money," as if they should be able to focus on higher causes while their children are hungry, without even wondering if their participation in ministry might help with their material needs.

Ironically, the remarks we make, even facetiously, when a millionaire philanthropist is mentioned show that we are the same when our role is reversed. If we know a person is a millionaire, we can't help but hope he will notice our ministry efforts and needs and feel like giving. We may even make sure he sees some demonstration or hears some details that might put the idea in his mind. Yet we look down on those who are financially below us when they do the same.

---

27 Corbett and Fikkert, 53.

If you were without basic essentials, and a generous, wealthy person were around, what would you be doing?

It's easy to see the disdain that is shown when a person throws a coin on the ground for someone to pick up, but often our giving carries unintended meaning.

A white missionary was known for bringing a bag of candy to give out when he visited the conventions in a Caribbean country. There was excitement the afternoon when he was going to give it out. To make it even more fun, he stood on a balcony and had the people, children and adults, to gather below. From the balcony he threw the bags of M & M's for the black people below to catch.

A homeless woman was eating with a pastor's family. The pastor's wife had a habit of sometimes tossing a biscuit to someone who was out of reach. During the meal, the pastor's wife offered the woman a biscuit, then casually tossed it to her. The homeless woman was deeply offended at what seemed to her to be contemptuous treatment. She later said, "She threw that biscuit to me like I was a dog or something."

> **"She threw that biscuit to me like I was a dog or something."**

A salesman walked into an inner-city church and found the pastor there. He offered to produce a church directory for the congregation. Photographers would come to take pictures of each family; then the photos would be printed in a directory with whatever other information the church provided. It would be done at no cost to the church or members. The company provided the service hoping to be able to sell additional photographs to the families participating. The pastor explained to the salesman that the congregation was poor, but the salesman insisted that it was no problem.

The great day arrived, the photographers set up their studio, and families came for their appointments. However, the photographers became frustrated after the second appointment. They were not selling much. They realized that the whole day would be a series of families that would be poor customers. They mentioned that they might pack up and leave, but the pastor held them to their agreement. They began pushing families through with a quick snapshot style, and at the end of the day packed and left without photographing the last family scheduled.

Sometimes a person being helped tries to retain his dignity by not appearing desperate and by not thanking the benefactor profusely. He may even try to act like he barely needed the help. The giver sometimes mistakes this as ingratitude rather than realizing that the recipient is trying to avoid the humiliating image of being desperately dependent. If the giver pushes for expressions of gratitude, the recipient may feel that the giver is just trying to make him admit his lower status and inadequacy.

One pastor asked a woman who failed to thank him for help, "If I had not come, who would you have called?" He just wanted to be appreciated, but she immediately caught the significance of the question and was angry. She resented the implication that she was without options.

An old saying is that "beggars can't be choosers." For example, a person who is hungry and cannot pay should take what is offered without complaining or even expressing preferences. But do we really understand what it feels like to be begrudged of even the basic dignity of being able to say what we want?

Two college students were taking a little girl home after a children's service. They noticed that she didn't have socks. They stopped by a store and bought socks for her. When they arrived at her house, her mother saw what had happened and was furious. The double offense was that they had assumed her inability to provide for her daughter and had taken that role without even asking her.[28] Imagine the feelings of impoverished parents everywhere when others come in and do for their children what they cannot do.

Many impoverished parents dread Christmas, because they cannot even come close to meeting the gift-buying expectations of the culture they live in. If some organization brings gifts to their house and gives them directly to their children, they feel their inadequacy even more. This travesty can be avoided if benefits to children are provided through their parents. Best of all is when the parents are provided the opportunity to earn and choose what their children receive.

The "Sponsor"

Clive Cussler told the story of a salvage operation at sea that he financed. As he and the crew boarded the ship, it was raining, and he struggled aboard with his luggage, without help. To correct what he saw as an inappropriate attitude, he stopped them and made a speech. He held up his hand and said, "Look, everyone, this hand is the most important thing here. Always take care of this hand. Even if the ship goes down, save this hand." A crewman naturally asked, "What's so important about that hand?" Cussler said, "This is the hand that writes the checks." After that, he got the attentiveness that he thought he deserved.

In the business world, the one with capital owns the business and is more important than anyone else. He makes the

---

28 Told by Randy White in *Encounter God in the City*.

decisions, even deciding what everyone else receives. That attitude often carries over to ministry. The sponsor calls the shots rather than decisions being made with all the right people participating.

> ## Mission churches tend to have an "us and them" mentality.

Mission churches tend to have an "us and them" mentality; the people on the ministry team constantly distinguish themselves from the people being served. They hold meetings and times of fellowship that do not include any of "them." But people do not want to be considered projects or patients.

"Since one does not go to the doctor when he is well, curing, then, cannot long serve as the basis of any relationship that is life-enhancing for both participants."[29] If we go into ministry with a focus on curing or changing people, we do not enter real fellowship with them.

Giving is actually a hindrance to fellowship when it takes control of the relationship.

A mission director was buying some small items at a grocery store in the Dominican Republic. As they came to the cashier, a local pastor under his supervision insisted on buying the things for him. The director hesitated to accept, knowing that the pastor was in poverty compared to himself, but then he realized that the pastor wanted to make sure that their relationship was beyond the terms of a giver and recipient in fixed roles.

---

29 Robert Lupton, *Compassion, Justice, and the Christian Life*, Regal Books, Ventura, CA, 22.

The "Thank You" Exchange

The "thank you exchange" is when a transaction is made and each feels that he gained. One-way charity leads to greed, manipulation, sense of entitlement, and resentment on the part of the recipients.

A man who asked for special prayer at the end of an inner-city evangelistic service kept asking afterward what he could do to help or give. He was told that grace meant there was nothing he needed to do in return except spread the word. What he may have understood was that there was nothing he could do or give that had any value.

The pastor of an inner-city church was moving church pews with the help of Tony, a man from the community. When they needed more help, Tony recommended a man who could be hired, but did not accept pay himself because he wanted to be considered part of the ministry.

One-way giving causes the giver to despise the recipients, and the recipient to resent the role he is fixed in. This often explains the ingratitude and rudeness displayed by recipients.

We categorize people as needy, permanent recipients, and often recognize them at first sight. When we fail to ask for their help, or especially when we turn down their offers, we are telling them that they have nothing to offer that we want in return.

> **We categorize people as needy, permanent recipients.**

Blame

It is impossible to totally separate blame from responsibility, for if we imply that a person is in the problem in spite of all he could have done, we imply that he may be powerless to change. That puts the solution in someone else's hands, and leaves him in the position of waiting for someone to do something for him.

But instead of focusing on blame and emphasizing past mistakes, it may be possible to emphasize going on from where you are.

The key questions for establishing responsibility are "Whose problem is this?" "Who is able to solve it?" "Who must make the choices?"

Whenever help seems to be necessary, the question should be asked, "What kind of help will let the recipient begin to make his own decisions and take responsibility for his future?" Any help that does not bring the needy person toward responsible freedom will probably only prolong his dependency.

Distorted Dignity

We see the desperate search for dignity and significance in such extremes as youth rebellion, graffiti, and joyriding.

A man who strolls across the street, making cars wait for him, is grasping for a sense of significance. He is making those drivers acknowledge his importance.

Sometimes the craving for dignity cripples a person from doing what he could to gain significance to others, because the path of service seems to go the wrong direction. He refuses to perform menial work because it would seem to be giving up what self-respect he has left, but it would actually increase his value.

Many cannot keep a job because they cannot take orders or criticism at work.

A woman stopped preparing coffee for the Sunday school class she attended because others did not leave the pot clean for her. A man refused to mop at a place where he had been getting free meals. Ironically, menial tasks get passed upward to those of acknowledged higher status, because they are secure and do not mind serving, and have the greater purpose in view.

Dignity in Development

The value of dignity should guide not only our occasional giving but our approach to helping people develop. Even when it seems obvious that help is needed, we must consider what the unintended results of our help may be.

The emergency or "relief" approach continuously applied to ongoing conditions creates dependency.

Never do for someone what he could do for himself. It's a temptation to do something for him that he should be doing so he can see the results he could be getting. But if a butterfly is assisted in coming from the cocoon, he is permanently damaged. If a chicken is helped to

> **Never do for someone what he could do for himself.**

hatch, he may never walk. A person must have full responsibility for his rate of progress. We offer opportunities, but we must not relieve a person of the essential discipline of personal development.

Ask, "What do you need to do so that you won't need our help one year from now?" (Wayne Gordon - Lawndale's question).[30] Then help them set an accountable plan of action.

Benjamin Franklin said, "Experience runs a dear [expensive] school, but a fool will learn in no other." To learn by expe-

30 John Fuder, ed. *A Heart for the City.*

73

rience is to learn by consequences. To take away the consequences of a person's actions is to take from him his last chance to learn. Just as importantly, it takes from him the freedom to make real decisions.

If done properly, they will someday say, "We have done it ourselves." The wrong kind of help can permanently hinder self-value and independence.

Chapter 11
Responsibility-Based Help

So whose fault is it, anyway? And who could change it? The second question seems more positive and forward-thinking than the first, but the topic of blame cannot be completely avoided as we try to identify who can change things.

One writer tackled the issue of responsibility this way:

> ...the source of collective inner-city struggle is not due in any way to personal failings, the force of nature, a lack of collective activity by the community, the presence of neighborhood 'pathology,' a lifestyle of sin, or any deficiencies in character or moral behavior. A lack of personal responsibility did not build the inner city. Instead, a historically accurate understanding of the inner city requires us to see inner-city neighborhoods as created by institutionalized racism, economic exclusion, and adverse political determinations.[31]

The first sentence of this quote is a sweeping generalization. Notice that the writer says that the problem is "not due in any way" to the things he listed, which include most of the apparent causes of inner-city problems.

If he is right, certain implications follow. People of the inner city are totally powerless and totally dependent on outside deliverers. Their failures did not get them there, and their efforts will not solve their problems. There is no message to take to them except to cooperate with efforts on their behalf. Most of the battle will take place elsewhere, since conditions are caused by "institutionalized racism, economic exclusion,

---

31 Mark R. Gornik, *To Live in Peace: Biblical Faith and the Changing Inner City*, 50.

75

and adverse political determinations." Their position would be similar to that of prisoners whose release must be negotiated elsewhere while they wait for someone to come and open the doors. To take all blame away from the poor might seem to be a way of giving respect, but it actually does the opposite by taking from them the ability to act, and by shifting the focus to outside decision makers.

> **The plight of the poor is not to be solved by affirming their helplessness.**

The need to legislate, lobby, and advocate for justice is great. But to emphasize that need by minimizing the choices of the person in need is a mistake. The plight of the poor is not to be solved by affirming their helplessness, but by making their decisions significant.

Empowerment

The concept of empowering the poor does not mean the same thing to everyone. To some it means bringing back to the poor the rights that have been taken from them, lifting them from their helplessness. That is an important part of poverty alleviation, often neglected, but another aspect of empowerment is also important and neglected.

The following was quoted previously: "Poor people typically talk in terms of shame, inferiority, powerlessness, humiliation, fear, hopelessness, depression, social isolation, and voicelessness. North American audiences tend to emphasize a lack of material things such as food, money, clean water, medicine, housing, etc."[32] This leads to misguided efforts.

---

32 Corbett and Fikkert, 53.

Empowerment of the poor is to recognize that the key to their circumstances is in their own hands. Any assistance brought to them that does not find a place in their plan for themselves will mostly be wasted.

Some organizations seek to simply transfer to the poor all the resources they need. No effort or decision-making is desired from the recipients. The goal is to give them food, water, education, shelter, and everything else they need for quality life. Because resources are ultimately limited, this kind of assistance is difficult to sustain, and may cause trauma when it abruptly ends.

But if total external support of an impoverished community were achieved, it would destroy the most important human need. A person may be healed of a disease without his understanding or even against his will, but an impoverished person cannot be taken out of poverty without his understanding and purposeful cooperation, unless he is put into a role similar to that of an animal in a zoo.

The poor themselves are already conscious of their basic need of empowerment, but many efforts of poverty alleviation ignore that need. Communities that have received the most assistance typically have two apparently contradictory characteristics; they complain that they are not getting enough, and they resent the dependent role that has been assigned to them.

> **The poor themselves are already conscious of their basic need of empowerment.**

Emergency Response Versus Development

"One of the biggest mistakes that North American churches make—by far—is in applying relief [emergency response] in situations in which rehabilitation or development is the appropriate intervention."[33] Ministries and government agencies respond to needs as if they are emergencies, but some of these emergencies have gone on for fifty years.

Poverty creates emergency situations, but to always respond to needs as if the needy person is totally helpless and needs urgent, unquestioning assistance is to build his dependency.

The story is told of a man who sent his grown sons to help a new neighbor chop trees for building a house. He gave his sons these instructions: "Chop while he is chopping. If he stops to talk or rest, you stop also, and when he quits for the day, come home."

It's always a bad sign when outsiders have traveled in at their own expense to help build while the men of the place who will be benefited by the project sit and watch. Do they not agree that the work should be done? Do they think it is worth the effort of others but not effort of their own? Will they commit any effort to maintaining it when it is finished? Are they likely to cash it in somehow to get something else that they care about more?

A Fable

George and Sam were brothers, but were not much alike. George quickly showed strong character and a sense of responsibility, while Sam never seemed to have either. George finished his education, advanced his career, and raised a family, while Sam accumulated debt, addictions, and a criminal record. Sam would never own a home or have a stable income. George sometimes struggled financially, but he tried to take care of

---

33 Corbett and Fikkert, 105.

Sam. He bought the house next door to his own for Sam to live in. The utilities were in George's name, since they would never be kept on otherwise. He checked on Sam daily and made sure he got enough to eat. He required Sam to work a few hours per week in his shop. This was for Sam's benefit rather than George's, since his unreliability and lack of skill cost more than his work was worth. Occasionally people noticed Sam's poverty and contributed. Ironically, they always gave the money to Sam, who had never spent a dollar wisely, while George continued his effort at his own expense.

> # You don't help the most by helping those who need help most. You help the most by helping those who will do the most with the help.

Concepts and Principles

The following paragraphs present various concepts and illustrations for consideration.

Some social workers assume that nobody would be impoverished by choice. While it is true that nobody wants to be without the things he needs, many aspects of the lifestyle of poverty are matters of choice. It is reality that many want their financial situation to change but are unwilling to change the things that create it. It's as though a person says, "I do not want to work, but I have the right to be provided with the products of work." Or, "I don't want to maintain a faithful, tolerant relationship with anyone, but I want others to be ready to help me when I need them."

It makes you wonder, "Would there be as many people who leave their relatives' house with angry words and a door slam and walk out into the snow if there were not government-subsidized shelters for those who have burned all their bridges?"

Let's look at an extreme illustration. If a person fell into a pit, we would see the immediate need of getting him out. But imagine that he has been there so long that he thinks he will never get out. His first request may not be that you get him out but that you bring him something to eat. You may respond to that need first, assuming that the next immediate goal is for him to get out, but he may not assume the same. He may ask for more things to make him more comfortable in the pit, and soon he needs to eat again. Finally, you will say, "Look, I'm here to help you get out of the pit; I'm not here to make you comfortable in the pit, and I'm not going to keep wasting time on that."

Misguided assistance leads to a poverty compounded by dependency and hopelessness. It is not a charitable act to support self-destructive habits when we would refuse to do the same for our own children. If your child was on the street with a sign asking for money, would you give him a dollar?

Loading a depressed neighborhood with human services may be the very approach that keeps it from recovering. For example, if a neighborhood has few home owners, does it really need more subsidized apartment buildings? Do we not understand what happens to a neighborhood when nobody who lives there owns anything?

There is actually something called the homeless industry, where organizations live on donations that come because they are meeting the needs of the homeless. It is not in the best interest of those who work in the homeless industry for the needs of the homeless to end.

Sure, teach a man to fish, but even better, teach him how to own the pond. In Micah 4:4, for a man to have his own vine and fig tree was prosperity. Private property and private enterprise are necessary to prosperity and security, as well as to dignity. Capitalism, whatever its faults, has proved one thing beyond dispute: when a person owns a means of production, he will put incredible effort and creativity into making it succeed.

So for every building and enterprise for the poor, the question should be asked, "Who will own this?"

> **Teach a man to fish, but even better, teach him how to own the pond.**

The Little Red Hen

Among children's stories, "The Little Red Hen" is a classic. Not only is it a demonstration of character and responsibility, but it shows a Christian response to a social problem.

The little red hen got something right. First, when she found some wheat, she made the most of the opportunity. She could have just eaten the grain, but she saw its potential as seed.

The hen showed compassion on others by offering to share the opportunity. She gave the other animals the chance to participate in the work and share the rewards. She even offered them the chance to enter at various stages of the process.

Her invitation was an offer of partnership. Had they accepted, the working relationship could have been complicated. How to measure the work of each and to divide accordingly would have been one challenge. To decide how much need should be considered along with work value would have been another issue. However, the hen was willing to undertake the partnership relationship.

When the other animals turned down the opportunity, the hen felt no obligation to share the bread produced. She did not feel guilty because of having something they lacked, nor did she sympathize with their hunger. She had shown compassion the best way by offering to share the opportunity.

What can the church learn from her example? First, it is not enough that those who have resources give away some of them. Giving without relationship and responsibility puts no difference between those willing to work and those who are not, puts no value on the work they could have contributed, and develops in them a sense of entitlement, where they feel qualified to receive simply on the basis of need.

Instead, Christians in business should offer the needy an opportunity to take responsibility and share in the rewards of production. This distinguishes those who are willing to work from those who are not. They should not be treated the same.

Paul wrote to the Thessalonian church that "if any would not work, neither should he eat" (2 Th. 3:10). This direction implies something about the community that the church had. They were making sure that none of those in their fellowship were going hungry.

Paul told them to require everyone to work. To really do that would require more than just telling people to find a job. Not everyone is able to find and take one of the jobs available in the marketplace, but everyone can do something of value. The fact that the church could require work implies that they had work opportunities to offer.

Paul seems to be addressing a community that had both food and work available, telling them that they could and should require all to work.

So how should we respond to the innumerable financial needs that surround us? Not by careless distribution, nor even by distribution based on qualifications. Rather, it's a sharing of the opportunity to create resources, allowing the one with needs to take responsibility.

A visitor to Haiti brought boxes of sunglasses, intending to distribute them freely. Much to her shock, the missionary she was visiting sternly forbade her to do it and put the sunglasses into storage. Weeks later, the missionary was visited by a woman from the congregation who was discouraged because she was unemployed and without opportunities. The missionary asked her to take some of the sunglasses to the market and sell them. She did so, returning what he required of the money, and keeping a profit. He gave her more sunglasses, and the process was repeated several times until the sunglasses were all gone. When she found out there were no more, she was upset that the opportunity had ended. The missionary then said, "Wait, you have found that you can successfully sell things at the market; surely there are other things you could sell, and the money you brought me from the sunglasses can be used as starting capital." The plan worked, and the woman was able to build her business.

"Ministry to the needy" will look very different if we do it in the style of the little red hen.

Chapter 12
The Dignity of Work

If you were asked to describe the perfect lifestyle, how would you do it? Many people think that part of it would be to have enough money that they would never have to work.

But work was part of the perfect world God created. When the world first appeared, spoken into existence by the voice of God, it was exactly as He wanted. He made the first people exactly as He wanted them, and put them in the environment that would be perfect for them.

And God gave the first people jobs. He wouldn't have had to. He could have designed everything to go on so that there wasn't anything that they needed to do, but He didn't.

Part of perfection was for people to have jobs. A job doesn't necessarily mean being hired by someone. Adam wasn't hired by anyone, but he had a job.

In that perfect world there was much that was different from the way it is now. Everything was in harmony. Plants were not stricken with diseases. The soil was rich without fertilizer being added. Many things were growing that produced food without anything being done to get them started and keep them going.

> **God designed nature to be at its best under human administration.**

But even with things like they were, there was a job for Adam and Eve to do. God designed nature to be at its best under human administration.

Humans are in a special relationship to creation. We are above the rest of nature because something of the nature of God is in us.

Sometimes people who are concerned about the environment think that people are just part of nature and have no right to change anything. They seem to think people are no more important than the spotted owl or the tree frogs. One family was not allowed to build their house because a pair of eagles had built a nest close to where the house was to be built.

But God gave people the authority and responsibility to manage the earth, bring it under control, and develop it. That has led to the development of all branches of agriculture, raising of animals, development of breeds, mining minerals out of the earth, and development of technology.

Has man always been responsible in what he did with the earth? Obviously not. Pollution, extermination of species, waste of resources, and development of technology for war are all things God did not intend. Those things are misuses of the responsibility God gave to man.

But nature responds to man's dominion, and when man is faithful to his responsibility, nature is better for it. An example is what has happened with the giant redwood trees in California.

These enormous trees took thousands of years to grow, which means if they were destroyed, they could not be replaced for a long, long time. A couple of the first Americans who found those trees chopped down the largest one they could find just to see how long it would take. Later lumberjacks began cutting them down for timber, but the trees tended to crack apart when they fell, so they didn't work out well for lumber. Otherwise, they would probably all be gone.

Eventually, people realized that the trees needed to be protected. A national preserve was established. People were not allowed to disturb anything there, not cut anything, not make fires, only look. Then some new problems appeared. The underbrush got thick, and pine needles and leaves became so thick on the ground that no new trees were growing. Also, whenever there was a fire from lightning, there was so much accumulation of brush on the ground that the fire could hardly be put out, and it would burn up some of the big trees. People found that the best way to preserve the area was to cut out some of the extra undergrowth and have fires occasionally to burn up some of the accumulation on the ground.

So the first people there, acting irresponsibly, would have destroyed the trees. But when the trees were left totally alone they were not at their best either. Nature does better under the responsible administration of people.

Work is like creation. Work is the means of dominion over nature – work is man's way of reshaping his environment. Work is not just to earn a living. Adam did not have to work in order to have food. He would have had food anyway. Adam needed work not to earn what he needed to live, but to shape his part of the world.

People have the instinct to make changes to their environment. People landscape their yards. They paint and decorate rooms. They try to dispose of trash.

A person who no longer desires to work has given up his desire and ability to change his environment. He is giving up part of what it means to be human.

For some people, games take the place of work, because game playing is an imaginary environment where they can be significant.

But What If I Can't Get a Job?

In many places and times the whole concept of being hired was not for most people. They found a way to produce something by work. There have been societies based on farming, and people produced food and other things by their work. They had a concept of owning a means of production and working to produce.

Of course there were people hired to haul things for the producers or hired to sell things for the producers, but the ones who were secure were not the ones who were hired, but the ones who owned the means of earning. Instead of being hired to pick corn in someone's field, they had a field and raised corn. Instead of being hired to drive someone's truck, hauling someone's corn, they owned a truck to drive for people.

Before owning the pond, many people have to develop themselves. Otherwise you could be your own worst employee. Instead of complaining that nobody wants to hire you, consider the kind of job you have done so far for yourself.

> **You could be your own worst employee.**

A nationwide survey asked businesses what qualities they wanted to see in welfare recipients who applied for entry-level positions. The survey listed twelve qualities, and asked which three were most important.

One of the qualities in the list of twelve was training; another was prior work experience; another was dressing appropriately.

You might be surprised what businesses said were the three most important qualities. Training was chosen by only 4% of the employers. Prior work experience was chosen by only 12%. Only 10% chose dress.

Instead, 66% looked for a positive attitude about the job. Reliability was wanted by 66%. A strong work ethic was wanted by 39%. And coming in at fourth place, punctuality was important to 31%. Of course being punctual is really part of being reliable and having a strong work ethic.

What people really get hired for is their view of work. What do you really think of work? What is your attitude about work? The main factor for getting hired is what the employer thinks you think about work.

And God Cares What You Think About Work.

If you think it is something to avoid, or something to endure when you have to, like taking medicine when you are sick, you do not have the right view of work. Adam did not have to work to survive, but he worked because it was part of God's perfect design for humanity.

It seems really significant that God has designed for so much to depend on work. He could have just given us everything we need for survival and let us spend our time on entertainment and friends and learning interesting things. Instead, survival depends on work; everything we have is produced by work, and our surroundings are maintained and improved only by work.

People have to learn to cooperate, depend on each other, be reliable for one another, use strengths and help others with weaknesses, meet challenges together, work out disagreements, correct mistakes, be faithful to people they will never meet, be trained, and train others.

God designed work because we need it. To help a person escape from work is not doing him a favor. The fact that work was part of the perfect world shows that it should not be viewed as a bad thing. Work is not just for people who can't survive some other way. It is not enslavement by people who have the money and can hire others to do their work for them.

Most rich people work longer hours than other people. Why? Because they want to be even richer? It's not so much the desire to get more money as it is the fulfillment of continuing to create, and move things, and impact their world.

> **To help a person escape from work is not doing him a favor.**

Working does not mean that you are insignificant; work is a means of finding significance. Work does not mean that you are not free. Work is a free relationship that you enter in order to do things that you want. The person who will not work because he wants to be free can hardly buy a can of pop unless someone else gives him "permission" by giving him some money. To be without any responsibility is usually to be without any freedom.

Mahatma Gandhi said, "What you do may seem insignificant, but it is most significant that you do it." Let's imagine a man who sweeps floors to make a living. That may seem like an insignificant job, but consider the choice he is making. When he decides to go to work every day, he is choosing to do that rather than spend his time idly with no value to anyone. He is choosing to take responsibility for supporting himself rather than being a parasite on friends or family. He is taking care of those who are depending on him, perhaps a wife and children, rather than forcing them to look for help. All those considerations give weight to the statement that while the work itself may seem insignificant, it is significant that he does it.

If people saw work as fulfilling and significant they would not choose a job just because of what it pays. They would also not envy those who are merely entertainers (who often take up some cause searching for significance themselves). They would not yield to the temptation to do something evil for income.

The person frying hamburgers at Burger King is much more significant than the drug dealer, because he is meeting real needs instead of destroying people. He also has put effort into personal development. The very fact that he is there shows that he has learned self-control, and he successfully faces challenges to his character every day. When frustrations come, he resists the temptation to throw down his apron and walk out because he knows that more important things are at stake. That is not weakness but strength. The drug dealer is letting his character and personality get erased, gradually obliterated, by yielding to all his weaknesses and calling that freedom.

If the work available is not what you would prefer, there are some things to remember. As a Christian, the first purpose is to serve, to become valuable by meeting needs. Remember that you are to work as though your employer is God. Remember that God is in control of promotion and rewards faithfulness in His time.

What does it mean to serve? It's to bring your abilities, benefits, and advantages to the one you serve. It is to set aside some of your rights and privileges; for example, you may not be able to sleep as late as you want in the morning, and you cannot spend work time doing what you want to do. You subordinate aspects of your life to a purpose you are hired for. Employment even affects the way you dress and the way you treat other people.

Look what we see about an employed person. He is dressed to some code that has been given him, or at his best. He is often hurrying to get somewhere. He has to plan his schedule, because his time has value. He is moving with purpose. He is not available all the time; he has a bedtime; he has a rising time. His unemployed friends may joke about how he is not free anymore.

But there are things moving in his life; he has plans, he is buying things; he is improving his conditions. He has some big goals that he never would have thought of before.

Then one morning at about 10:00 you see him sitting on his porch drinking coffee. Late at night you see the flickering of his television. He now wears whatever he wants. He is in no hurry; he is available for whatever he wants to do. But things are no longer moving in his life; he has few plans because he has few options.

Some people persist in their refusal to serve as their last clutch on dignity. They have little to be proud of, but they cling to self-sovereignty. "I don't have to let people treat me wrong, boss me, control me." They may be quick to take offense or make a big deal out of something little as a way to show their grip on dignity and personal value; they demand to be accounted for.

Because they don't have the dignity of work, they clutch at dignity in ridiculous ways. A person who is forced to perform some task may do it slowly and poorly. A person like that is just showing that he does not

> **Doing something cheerfully and well shows freedom because nobody could make you do that.**

have freedom. Doing something cheerfully and well shows freedom because nobody could make you do that.

91

As an employee, if your main priority is to make sure you are not a servant, you will not long be an employee. Proving that you do not serve just proves that you cannot make yourself valuable to others.

Look at the example of a grocery store manager. His priority is to sell items and keep everything running smoothly. One afternoon he notices a puddle of cooking oil where someone knocked a bottle off the shelf. The nearest employee is Albert, so he tells him to clean it up.

But Albert thinks that the main priority of the store is to guard his rights and dignity. He complains that the customer shouldn't have left it; the previous employee shouldn't have left it, and an employee in that section should do it.

Imagine another employee named Carl. He is good at seeing what needs to be done. He cleans up spills without waiting to be told; he restocks shelves when he sees them empty, and he is quick to notice a customer that needs help. Actually he works as though his priority is to keep the store selling and running smoothly, the same priority the manager has.

Of course, Carl gets taken advantage of sometimes. Other employees leave messes or unfinished duties. Sometimes Carl is called in early or held late.

But everyone knows that Carl knows where things are and how everything is to be done. When they need a shift super-visor, Carl gets the job.

It's not because of how long he has been there. It's not because he needs the money. Actually, the manager was not trying to do something for Carl by promoting him; he was doing something for himself, because he needs Carl.

Let's imagine that someday Carl is the general manager of the store. It is now his job to do whatever it takes to make sure everything gets done. Coming in to open he straightens a display and puts away the mop bucket that someone left out. He worked late the night before in place of a sick shift manager, then did product orders. Whatever has to be done is his job if someone else doesn't do it.

Carl obviously can't do everything, so he observes whom he can ask to do things, who remembers without being checked up on. If the employee could just realize it, being asked to do extra is an honor. He watches for people that share the store's priorities and makes them shift managers.

Much of the day he is in his office dealing with problems that most people don't know exist. Maybe an advertised item didn't arrive on the truck. The tuna fish all needs to be pulled because something is wrong with it, and some has been sold already. A customer slipped on the ice outside and is threatening to sue.

Meanwhile Albert is sitting across from him, saying, "I shouldn't have to clean up that puddle; that isn't my job." It's not going to take Carl long to realize that his job would be easier if he didn't have Albert.

For churches that share life together, there is a lot of work to be shared. Imagine that after a congregational meal, when it comes time to mop, one of those asked to mop is Albert. He comes back and says, "The mop bucket is full of dirty water, and the mop is sitting in it." "Well," says the pastor, "just empty the bucket and rinse the mop and run fresh water." Albert objects, "I shouldn't have to do that; whoever used it should have done that."

Thoughts the pastor might have about Albert: "You got up this morning and had nothing to do but dress yourself and wait to be picked up. You were brought here in a van you didn't have to pay for or maintain, on roads you didn't have to help with (since you don't pay taxes), to a building you don't pay for, ministered to freely by people here, ate a meal you didn't pay for or help cook—and you are afraid someone else is not taking enough responsibility? You want to make sure you don't do something someone else should have done? Don't worry, Albert, it will be done by someone willing to serve. Probably by one of the people who are already the busiest, helping you.

Chapter 13
Common Miracles

Suppose late one summer you walked into your back yard and found that a large section of it had grown tomatoes, corn, beans, and other great vegetables, and there was enough to last you for a long time.

Would that seem like a miracle? It happened to thousands of people last summer. They walked into their backyards and found all that growing and even more.

But they weren't amazed, or even surprised, because a few months before, they had cultivated the ground, then planted seeds in it, then for months made sure it was watered and weeded. So when they found a crop growing, it was only what they expected.

You may react, "Then that wasn't a miracle at all." But God made millions of plants, and man has never made one.

Psalm 104:14 says, "He causes the grass to grow for the cattle, and herbs [vegetables] for the service of man, that he may bring forth food out of the earth." God does it, but man prepares for it by preparing the ground, planting seeds, and watering when necessary.

A lot of people think of an act of God as something unusual, an exception to natural law, such as when Jesus healed or when the sun stood still. So in that sense, plants growing are not miracles because they are ordinary.

But in wishing for a miracle, we too often skip over God's normal way of doing things. We wish for the extraordinary and miss the opportunity to receive the benefits of God's normal operation.

> **We wish for the extraordinary and miss the opportunity.**

There were millions of people who walked into their back yards and did not find anything growing that they could eat. They did not get involved in that way that God has of producing food.

But food growing is just one example of God's normal work. Maybe that one is not for you, but there are others that everyone needs to be involved in.

For example, God's normal way of providing for needs is through work. "In all labor there is profit."[34] "An idle soul shall suffer hunger."[35]

There are people who wish God would provide something for them, but they pass up opportunities to work because it's not what they want to do. Some work is boring; some work gets you dirty.

And what if you are disabled, or you are looking for work, and willing to work, but you haven't found it yet?

There is work that you can do to help others, and through that work, some of your needs can be met. If you are unemployed, you have time, right? Why not look around and see what you can do to help someone else?

There is a spiritual principle of thinking of the needs of others and not being totally absorbed in your own needs. There is also a practical principle. Remember, those who hire people are not usually doing it to help them. They hire someone

---

34 Proverbs 14:23.
35 Proverbs 19:15.

because they think that person can meet a need that they have. So if a person is only able to think of what he wants somebody to do for him, he may not be worth hiring.

What if you can begin to form a new mindset – looking for ways to serve others?

Willis stopped by a church to ask for money. A group of men, including the pastor, were unloading a truck. As they went back and forth carrying heavy loads, Willis walked back and forth with them, empty handed, explaining why he needed money.

JFK's famous statement was, "Ask not what your country can do for you; ask what you can do for your country." That is hard for some people to do, whether it's their country, or church, or friends. But a Christian should think that way.

There are all kinds of benefits of that mindset.

(1) Jesus said, "It is more blessed to give than to receive." Do you really believe that? Do you live like you believe it?

(2) It forms relationships that will result in some of your needs being met. Often this happens in unpredictable ways, so it's not just a matter of helping the people that you think will be able to do something for you.

(3) It will help you to find a valuable place in the church, the body of Christ.

(4) It may develop you into a person that someone would want to hire. A person may say, "Well, I would be friendly and helpful and honest if I were getting paid for it," but employers don't hire an unfriendly person and pay him to be friendly. They don't hire a dishonest person and pay him to be honest. They are looking for a friendly, helpful, and honest person to hire.

In the church things are different. We don't wait for a person to give or be friendly before we are willing to help him. God also reaches out to you and blesses you before you do anything good. But for your own benefit, you need to start responding to grace. Learn to give and serve and smile.

Things happen when people are willing to work, willing to serve. Those benefits are things that would seem like miracles if they just happened unexpectedly, but God has a normal way of bringing those benefits into your life.

> **A person who doesn't learn these things thinks that a blessed person is lucky.**

It's probably a waste of time to be hoping, wishing, or even praying for God to do some miracle like having a bundle of money thrown to you, if you are not willing to receive help the way God likes to give it. A person who doesn't learn these things thinks that a blessed person is lucky.

Young man, young lady – will it be a miracle if someone someday gives you a high-paying job? That happens to some people, and like the garden, it is not a surprise, but prepared for and expected.

There are some characteristics that the person usually has who gets a good job that he can make a career out of.

He finished school; he got decent grades; he didn't get a criminal record; he stayed off of drugs, and he is not covered with tattoos. By the way, your appearance matters. When some people walk into a store, they look like the kind of person the security guard needs to watch, not a person the manager would want to hire.

Don't close the doors on your future by foolish actions. There are things you can be doing that will open doors. Then, when you go to the personnel office of a company, they say, "Oh, you could do this or this or this... ." You have options.

There are things that close your doors. Then you are talking to a counselor who is trying to help you find a career, and he says, "Here are fields you can't go into because you didn't study your math and science. Here's a list of fields you couldn't be trained for because you never read a book – just watched TV every waking moment. And you can't have a job dealing with people because you swear and get mad easily. You can't have a job handling money because you have a drug problem. And you can't learn a skill because you don't like for anyone to tell you what to do and tell you when you are doing it wrong."

How many opportunities does that leave?

God wants to do miracles in your life, but He has some usual ways that He likes to work. Don't wait to be disappointed that nothing good grew in your life because you didn't plant the seeds.

Chapter 14
Forgetting Poverty

A glance at poverty may give us the impression that the needs are obvious. There are people who lack the resources to get for themselves sufficient food, shelter, health care, education, and safety. The automatic response of a generous, compassionate person is to find a way to provide for the impoverished person something that he needs.

It is an undeniable fact that providing for the basic needs of a poor person does not remove him from poverty. If the help is not changing his situation, it will return him to his problems when it ceases.

> **Providing for the basic needs of a poor person does not remove him from poverty.**

A poor person may have trouble defining poverty or identifying the solution. His effort and planning is usually short- sighted, maybe even focused only on getting what he needs today. Therefore, he thinks he knows what he needs, but if he gets it, his situation will not change.

Some givers try to improve their effectiveness by looking for the causes of poverty that need to be corrected. This can also be a mistake.

"To seek 'causes' of poverty in this way is to enter an intellectual dead end because poverty has no causes. Only prosperity has causes."[36] So poverty automatically exists where the causes of prosperity are missing. Long-term strategy should not

---

36 Jane Jacobs, *The Economy of Cities*, 121.

aim at providing what people are lacking; that relieves poverty temporarily but does not bring prosperity. Instead, we should aim at mobilizing the causes of prosperity, and that will ultimately relieve poverty.

Instead of asking, "Why do these people not have enough food?" ask "Why do some people have enough food?" Forget about poverty long enough to look at its replacement. Look for causes of prosperity that can be replicated in places of need.

So poverty automatically exists where the causes of prosperity are missing.

Then give strategically in the way that will ultimately meet the most needs. That means that you don't invest in those who need it most, but in those who will do the most with it.

Getting the impoverished person to do long-range planning and change of direction has at least three obstacles. First, he is unused to thinking that way. Secondly, he is doubtful that it is possible to make things happen further into the future. Thirdly, he needs a way to support himself in the present while he works on something that will support him later.

For example, hunger does not motivate a person to plant a crop, because (1) he has not learned to provide for hunger so far in advance, (2) he does not think that his efforts will produce a crop, and (3) a future harvest cannot be eaten now.

The person with immediate needs must have temporary relief combined with a means of erecting the structure for bringing about prosperity. The lack of either usually causes failure of the benevolent effort.

Two concepts to establish (along with arranging temporary relief) are the concepts of functioning resources and asset inventory.

Functioning Resources

Because of not practicing planning and the building of a personal infrastructure, a poor person may not understand the concept of functioning resources. For example, he may assume that any person who has an expensive set of tools, or a computer, or a vehicle has plenty of money because if he were desperate he could sell them. However, any of those things may be a functioning resource that cannot be cashed without dropping a person into dependence.

If a person does not understand how functioning resources work for others, he probably does not know what resources would similarly work for him.

He may not be able to say exactly what he most needs or what kind of help would change his condition. He may describe help in terms of an immediate, brief boost in his daily efforts, rather than a real change of life.

Hunger does not motivate a person to plant a crop.

One aspect of poverty is the lack of functioning resources. Unless the person in poverty can learn the necessity of maintaining and reserving functioning resources, he cannot be brought out of dependence.

Asset Inventory

Asset inventory is to take a look at the resources that do exist in the impoverished community. Invariably there are resources that have been overlooked or undervalued. For example, unemployed people and abandoned buildings are resources that would be considered extremely valuable in some places, so how can they be made valuable where they are?

Asset mapping starts from a perspective that is opposite to listing needs. A focus on need moves quickly to list the things that must be brought in, tending to ignore what is there already. It is likely to come up with a program that will fail to thrive in the surroundings.

The process of asset inventory includes a lot of listening to the people involved. Sometimes outsiders think the needs are obvious, but there may be some part of the infrastructure missing that is not so obvious.

Chapter 15
The Call to the City

Trish and her small boy lived in a homeless shelter for several months. She became part of an inner-city church, shared life with them, and spent time in their homes. She found employment and was soon ready to look for a home to rent. The pastor was disappointed when he found out that she had rented an apartment on the other side of the city. He said, "I hoped you would be close enough to be involved with everything." She said, "Oh no, Pastor, I want to get out of that area!" With a sigh, he realized she was acting on the assumption that a "better life" always means "getting out."

As the city grows, those who can afford it move to the suburbs. Housing developments seem to spring up in the suburbs overnight, like little towns where the houses, streets, and parks are all new. New churches spring up there too, with names like Family Life Church or Valley Fellowship Church, drawing in the young or middle-aged couples who are upwardly mobile. Church planting models for the suburbs abound, and some of them work.

But the scene is different in the city. Within the beltway of most large cities are scores of neighborhoods where people live in poverty.

It seems ironic that when you leave "downtown" where banks and office buildings circulate millions of dollars every day and where a building site may be worth a million dollars, you have to go only a few blocks to be in the worst part of town where a house is difficult to sell at any price.

Neighborhoods of poverty are not only in the inner city that surrounds "downtown," however. They are throughout the city and may be streets where fine old homes have been divided into five apartments each, or where houses were built small and close together because of rising land costs, or where apartment complexes are government subsidized.

The scenery is ancient brick buildings, boarded-up windows, graffiti, potholes, broken sidewalks, and yards and vacant lots strewn with trash. The businesses that flourish are pawn shops, liquor stores, tattoo parlors, and check cashers. Sirens are heard several times a day. Gun shots are heard at night.

It's the area we call "the bad part of town." Sometimes people are driving and find themselves there by accident, and it isn't long before someone says, "We're in a bad part of town; let's get out of here." Just looking through a car window makes them feel that they are too close to people who are strange and may be dangerous.

And how are people who live in the area responding to the conditions around them?

One person's reaction to his neighborhood was to post a sign in his window that says, "No, no, no, this is not a mission; no, you can't use phone, no food, no money, no toilet, no ciga-rettes."

One church in the inner city kept their door locked even during services. There was a push button at the back seat that allowed entry. Whenever someone tried to enter, the person at the button would decide by the person's appearance whether or not it was safe to let him in.

Mission Neglect of the Cities.

What organizations do you know who are trying to plant churches in Philadelphia, Detroit, Louisville, Grand Rapids, Memphis, and Birmingham? New churches are being planted in prosperous suburbs, where the current church planting models work better.

Missionaries are sent to countries that have smaller populations than U.S. cities that we have not reached. There are 120 nations of the world that have smaller populations than the Detroit metro area.

Even on foreign mission fields church planting organizations tend to avoid the cities. Many missionaries have been sent to Mexico, but how many are in Mexico City, one of the world's largest?

It has not always been so, so why did we begin avoiding the city?

It is foreign. To many of those in ministry leadership, even American cities are foreign. Many of those entering the ministry have a small town or rural comfort zone.

We don't really know what lies behind graffiti, vandalism, food stamps, high school dropout rates, and signs that say, "Will work for food."

We are repelled by the city because it's where sin reveals itself at its worst with crime, addictions, and prostitution. It is where fallen humanity is found in its worst conditions of helplessness and hopelessness.

The city has danger, all the more intimidating because it is unfamiliar and exaggerated.

Cities are where humanity exalts itself in rebellion against God, starting with Cain, then Babel. They call forth from the fallen human heart reflections like those of Nebuchadnezzar, who was filled with pride as he surveyed what he had built.

Yet the kingdom of God can come in the city, and the grace of God can redeem it. After all, the ultimate destiny of the redeemed is not the Garden of Eden restored, but a city whose builder is God.

> **The kingdom of God can come in the city.**

Our heritage for city ministry goes all the way back to Jesus Himself, who grieved for the cities where He had ministered.

The Apostle Paul had a deliberate strategy for targeting cities for the sake of the whole region.

"[Paul was] disputing daily in the school of one Tyrannus. And this continued by the space of two years; so that all they which dwelt in Asia heard the word of the Lord Jesus, both Jews and Greeks."[37]

We can also observe that the majority of Paul's converts were from the poor. "For ye see your calling, brethren, how that not many wise men after the flesh, not many mighty, not many noble, are called . But God hath chosen the foolish things of the world to confound the wise; and God hath chosen the weak things of the world to confound the things which are mighty."[38]

Historically, great revival movements have had their greatest effects among the poor.

Why Should We Target the Cities with the Gospel?

(1) We have the precedent set by the Apostle Paul, who moved from one major city to another planting the gospel.

---

37 Acts 19:9-10.
38 1 Corinthians 1:26-27.

(2) There is a great heritage of urban ministry among the poor, especially represented by John Wesley and Methodism, then William Booth and the Salvation Army, and on to the evangelism of the American holiness movement that gave birth to some of the denominations that exist today.

(3) There is no limit to the potential spread of the gospel and growth of the church among the enormous populations in the city.

(4) Urban dwellers are less bound to tradition, less controlled by a previous culture, less prejudiced, and more open to new ideas.

(5) Effective, wide-spreading evangelism and revival have most often occurred among the poor.

(6) Cities are where new movements and ideas either win or lose, determining whether or not they penetrate the society.

(7) Mission fields are represented in the cities so much that a person could stay busy for a lifetime ministering to almost any foreign nationality in almost any major city.

Therefore...

Future foreign missionaries should be trained in urban ministry and plan to minister in cities.

Young people preparing for ministry should join a team that will target a specific city.

Churches, denominations, and mission boards must not just start rescue missions, soup kitchens, and homeless shelters, but plant the church in the heart of the city.

Resources Cited

Bakke, Ray. *A Theology as Big as the City*. Downers Grove, IL: IVP, 1997.

Bakke, Ray and Sharpe, Jon. *Street Signs: A New Direction in Urban Ministry*. Birmingham: New Hope Publishers, 2006.

Banfield, Edward C. *The Heavenly City Revisited*. Boston: Little, Brown, and Co., 1974.

Corbett, Steve and Fikkert, Brian *When Helping Hurts: How to Alleviate Poverty without Hurting the Poor and Yourself*. Chicago: Moody, 2009.

Dunstan, J. Leslie. *A Light to the City: 150 Years of the City Missionary Society of Boston, 1816, 1966*. Boston: Beacon Press, 1966.

Fuder, John. ed. *A Heart for the City: Effective Ministries to the Urban Community*. Chicago: Moody, 1999.

Gornik, Mark R. *To Live in Peace: Biblical Faith and the Changing Inner City*. Grand Rapids: Eerdmans, 2002.

Greenway, Roger S. and Monsma, Timothy M. *Cities: Missions' New Frontier*. Grand Rapids: Baker, 2000.

Jacobs, Jane. *The Economy of Cities*. New York: Vintage Books, 1968.

Lupton, Robert D. *Compassion, Justice, and the Christian Life*. Ventura, CA: Regal, 2007.

Marsden, George. *Fundamentalism and American Culture.* New York: Oxford University Press, 2006.

Perkins, John. *Beyond Charity: The Call to Christian Community Development.* Grand Rapids: Baker, 1993.

Phillips, Keith. *Out of Ashes.* Los Angeles: World Impact Press, 1996.

White, Randy. *Encounter God in the City: Onramps to Personal and Community Transformation.* Downers Grove, IL: IVP Books, 2006.